everyday
talk

everyday talk

TALKING FREELY *and* NATURALLY
about GOD *with* YOUR CHILDREN

JOHN A. YOUNTS

Shepherd Press
Wapwallopen, PA

© 2004 by Life*Is*Worship Publishing Group

Published by Shepherd Press
P. O. Box 24
Wapwallopen, PA 18660
www.shepherdpress.com
Printed in the United States of America

ISBN 0-9723046-9-X

Page design by Tobias' Outwear for Books.

Contents

Foreword 6

Introduction 7

Acknowledgments 9

1. Stupid Rain 11

2. Your Children and the Gospel 23

3. Listen to Your Children 32

4. Holy Directions 40

5. Don't Be Ordinary 55

6. Big Sins, Little Sins 66

7. Thirteen Comes Before Twenty-One 79

8. Your Home is God's Greenhouse 90

9. The World: The Grand Deception 97

10. Everyday Talk about Sex 110

11. Everyday Talk about Music 123

12. You are on Display 133

13. For Everything There is a Season 144

14. Conclusion 150

Foreword

Words have power. Successful preachers, hucksters and salesmen all know that. They have the power to transform the thoughts and lives of people—sometimes in radical and even dramatic ways. Hitler brought about World War II through haranguing the German people. And during the campaign for the 2004 election, which as I write is beginning at a feverish pace, the candidates are relying heavily upon speech. Today—more than at any other time in history—we live in a sea of speech.

Recognizing these facts, it is evident that the speech that we use in our families, before our children is an important matter. It is with that matter that Jay Younts deals in this book in depth. He is concerned not only with that which we consciously say to them, but also with that which they imbibe from our casual—and often thoughtless—conversation.

The book is an awakening call to those who have never given serious thought to the effect of their speech upon their children. But it doesn't only send a clarion call, it also provides direction for change. It shows the reader how to bring about good things through speech and guides him in dealing with poor habits of speech.

The book has been long in coming, and now that it has arrived the Christian community has a guide to an issue of utmost importance. Many families will be blessed by using it to help them in their desire to have loving, obedient children who serve the Lord.

— JAY ADAMS

Introduction

Once upon a time, many years ago, I was a child. Back in those days, we didn't have as much as kids do today. Styles didn't change as quickly, and wardrobes were simpler. I had only two pair of shoes. By today's standard, that's pretty minimal, but back then it wasn't unusual. I only needed two pair: one pair for Sunday and one pair for every other day.

Sunday shoes, like Sunday clothes, were worn on special occasions. Other than Sunday, we only used them for such events as weddings, funerals, and formal parties. Sunday shoes tended to be stiff and uncomfortable, but they looked good—and anyway, we never had to wear them too long. Back at home, we immediately changed into our everyday clothes and shoes.

Everyday shoes weren't "cool," as they are today. They were basic, neutral, go-with-everything shoes. Style was not an issue. I didn't think much about my shoes—I just wore them every day.

Everyday talk is like the everyday shoes of my childhood. It may not be attractive, but it's practical and gets the job done. We don't pay much attention to it.

On the other hand, we have "Sunday best" talk. When others are listening (especially Christians), we suddenly put on our best manners. We smile, chat pleasantly, and listen patiently. We are models of courtesy.

The problem is that everyday talk is far more important than "Sunday best" talk. It reveals us as we really are—our character and our priorities. Our children model our everyday talk because that is what they hear most of the time. By it we teach them our worldview, our ethics, our theology, and our relationship with God.

In the book of Deuteronomy, God says that everyday talk is a vital part of His plan for training children:

> These commandments that I give you today are to
> be upon your hearts. Impress them on your children.
> Talk about them when you sit at home and when you
> walk along the road, when you lie down and when
> you get up (Deuteronomy 6:6–7 NIV).

God is not just a Sunday God; He is for every day. If you live in awe of Him, your children will see that. If you love Him and serve Him, you will talk about Him every day, and your children will hear that. This book is written to help you understand and use the influence of your everyday talk on your children.

Shoes come and go. It doesn't matter at all what my everyday shoes were like when I was a child. But, everyday talk—that's different! The everyday talk that your child hears now will influence him for the rest of his life. My prayer is that this book will help you learn how God wants you to talk about Him every day.

Acknowledgments

It is all too true—this book has been long in coming. Many people deserve thanks for their contributions and encouragement.

In 1973 I read *Competent to Counsel* by Jay Adams. I still remember the excitement of reading about how the Bible could solve the problems of life. Seventeen years later the Lord moved my family to the church Dr. Adams started in Simpsonville, South Carolina. Jay encouraged me to begin writing. Through his preaching, writing and friendship Jay has held out the sufficiency of Christ's Word and the beauty of knowing and loving Jesus Christ. Jay's editing of this book has been invaluable.

The Lord has also used my friend, Tedd Tripp, to point me to the faithfulness of Christ. I met my wife in Tedd's home. For that, I could not be more thankful. I also saw in Tedd and his wife, Margy, how to follow Christ in parenting. I was blessed by God to watch Tedd's children grow up. Tedd, Heather and Aaron had much influence on my own children and on this book.

God blessed me with parents who loved Him and made that love a priority in my home. Austin and Pat Younts consistently believed in me and supported me through difficult times early in my adult life. Both Mom and Dad are with Him now, and I am grateful to God for their lives. My wife's parents have also been a wonderful encouragement. My father-in-law, Howard Long, was as passionate about his love for Christ as anyone I have ever met. His enthusiasm touched the lives of many across this country. He was a thinker who loved to show how the glory of God should dominate every aspect of life—not a bad legacy for a welding engineer! Genevieve, my mother-in-law, continues to be an example of selfless devotion to Christ. In her eighties now, she has the mind of a theologian and the spirit of servant.

Many helped make this book a reality with specific contributions. My brother, David, encouraged, counseled, and challenged me to complete this project. I also thank Bob and Mary Kay Land, who not only read the manuscript, but also provided encouragement to finish.

Many good friends have been used of God in various ways to help formulate the ideas that make up this book: Chris and Darla Reese, Greg and Berta Myers, Jon and Sue Oren, Rick and Bonnie Irvin, Greg and Harriet Strain, and James Lansberry. Larry, Valerie and Joshua Domagalski have been tremendous in their support and encouragement.

Thanks also to the elders of Redeemer Presbyterian Church in Moore, South Carolina, for providing me the opportunity to teach this material. Special thanks to Bill Slattery, my pastor and friend. I am grateful to the entire Redeemer Church community for their support.

I particularly want to thank Chris Tobias, a gifted graphic designer and good friend, for his dedication to Christ. Also, Patrick Fraley provided valuable insight, helping me to be more practical and clear.

My own children, Austin, David, Kaaren, Geneva and Ross, are the ones in whose lives the content of this book was forged. Some concepts in the book are the result of things that I did not do well as a father, things I learned after the fact. God has been faithful in spite of my weaknesses. I am thankful for each of my children and the encouragement they all are to me.

There is no way that I can adequately express my gratitude to my wife, Ruth. With regard to the book, she has been the principal editor, stylist and theological consultant. Her gifts of literary clarity and insight have turned a jumbled manuscript into its present form. She is also my friend and, in the fullest biblical sense, my helper. Thank you, Ruth.

Our sovereign Lord has brought all of these people and more into my life to provide the interactions by which the book has become a reality. The life of His Son has brought life and hope to me, and I pray that it will to you as well.

Stupid Rain

What is the most powerful human influence in your child's life?

Your "quality time" with your child?

Church and Sunday School?

Friends?

Parental discipline?

These may all be good things, but there is another influence more powerful than all of them. The most powerful personal influence in your child's life is **everyday talk**.

Everyday talk is talk that happens in the unplanned moments. It happens in casual, unguarded moments. It happens when you are distracted or irritated and would rather not be talking at all. It happens when you receive unexpected news, good or bad. You are always talking or thinking about things—at home or on the way to the mall, when you are driving to work or school, when you are falling asleep (or lying awake), or when you are dragging yourself out of bed in the morning. This is everyday talk.

The power of everyday talk

Talk is a given. Everyone talks. It's a basic function of life. In order to teach your kids you must talk to them. But there are all sorts of talk. For example, formal discussion (usually a monolog, in reality) occurs when you sit your children down and explain some matter that you think is really important. Then there is talk that gives directions, such as, "Take out the garbage," or "Be quiet," or "Come here." However, Deuteronomy 6 speaks about a specific type of talk that God wants you to have with your children—everyday talk.

Why do I say everyday talk is so powerful? Because the Bible teaches so.

Deuteronomy 6:6–7 says, "These commandments that I give you today are to be upon your hearts. Impress them on your children. Talk about them when you sit at home and when you walk along the road, when you lie down and when you get up."

The New Living Translation freely translates the same passage this way, "And you must commit yourselves wholeheartedly to these commands I am giving you today. Repeat them again and again to your children. Talk about them when you are at home and when you are away on a journey, when you are lying down and when you are getting up again" (NLT).

The kind of talk that God requires here is talk that happens in the normal routine of life, every day. God wants you to talk about His world. God wants you to talk about what He does and how people respond to Him. He wants you to do this when you are at home, when you are out and about, when you relax. He wants you to talk about Him with love and awe every day. He wants you to talk freely and naturally to your children about His commands and how to obey them day by day, hour by hour, minute by minute. This is what Deuteronomy 6:7 means. God wants your everyday talk to be about Him.

Does this idea seem strange or unnatural? Are you thinking, "What good will this do?" God's ways are not our ways.

Remember the historical setting of Deuteronomy. Moses was giving his final instructions to Israel before they were to enter into Canaan. Moses could not go with them. After leading them for forty years, he had to say goodbye and leave them to enter the Promised Land without him. He was giving Israel the tools and weapons they would need to overcome the Canaanites.

What weapon would enable them to conquer a land filled with ferocious warriors? It wasn't what you might expect. He told them to talk to their kids about God every day. In Deuteronomy 6:12, Moses told the Israelites not to forget about God when they entered the land. The way for the Israelites not to forget was *to talk to their children about God all the time*—when they got up or when they went to sleep, wherever they were. Talking about God and what He was doing for His people was to be a vital weapon against their enemies. It was the key to their success.

The weapon of everyday talk

Everyday talk is still key to successful parenting. But everyday talk is not automatically an effective weapon. At least two things have to happen. First, God says that *these commands of His are to be in your heart*, living there in a rich, full way. Think about that for a moment. Under the direction of the Holy Spirit, Moses says that these commands of God are to be so valuable to you that your heart cannot contain them. His commands are to dominate your thinking and overflow from your heart into the lives of your kids as you walk along life's road.

What kinds of thoughts live long enough in your heart to take up residence there? Or, said in a slightly different way, what things are so important to you that you can't stop thinking about them? Dads, how many times do you replay that six-iron that gave you a winning birdie? What about when your team won the big game in the last seconds? Is there a new car or new DVD player that is constantly on your mind? Are you consumed by getting your new fall wardrobe? Or, negatively, is your heart dominated by thoughts of how others have wrongly treated you? Are your thoughts dominated by how unfair life is? You get the point—what topics are alive inside your heart? What do your friends, family and coworkers hear about, whether they want to or not?

God wants his commands in that place of special privilege. Do you love God? Are you blown away by His Word? Is the awesomeness of God something that your mind keeps turning to? Does the sacrifice of Jesus on the cross for your sin dominate the thoughts of your heart? This is the picture of Deuteronomy 6 when it says, "These commands are to be upon your hearts." What thoughts live in your heart? You know and God knows. Your children know.

Second, impress them on your children. God wants you to repeat His Words over and over. Wherever you are with your children, they should hear about the constant interaction you are having with God and His Word. This is how God's word will make an impression on your children.

Lasting impressions cannot be made only by prayers at mealtime that thank God for food and missionaries and then nothing else is said about God until the next meal. Now, let me explain. This does not mean that you must quote the Bible all day, or spout systematic theology in every conversation. It does mean that as you grasp a profound truth of God's Word you will find ways to explain it to your children. Your knowledge and wisdom will become part of their lives, too.

For example, suppose you are reading in the Gospels and you come to passages where Jesus shows His power over the winds and the waves (Matthew 8:26–27). As you think about this you realize that God is so powerful that He controls the weather. All weather, everywhere. So when you see a cloud in the sky or experience a sudden, unexpected thunderstorm (even if it messes up your golf game), or read about a hurricane, you are amazed that Jesus is, indeed, Lord over the weather. You are blown away (pun intended) by the truth of Scripture. Talking about the weather isn't just small talk. Weather events are opportunities to talk to your children about God in the way that Deuteronomy 6 envisions. This insight isn't obscure or hard to understand—it's everyday talk!

God wants you to look at the world His way. You can learn to be thankful for a rainout. You can even learn to be intrigued at what God is doing. How many other events did He change by that thunderstorm? You are observing God at work! God wants you to use the ordinary events of life to teach your children to know and trust God and His Son.

Here is a practical example of this point.

Let's say you planned a special day. You scheduled this day weeks ahead. Today is the day. You were going to finish a landscaping project in the morning and then meet the guys for a round of golf at the country club. You had arranged to take the day off to get it all done. The forecast was for clear skies. But the growing puddles of rainwater spreading across the ground say the forecast was wrong. Your mood matches the dark clouds. You turn away from the window and mutter a comment about the stupid (or worse) rain.

"What, Daddy?"

Why couldn't it rain tomorrow?

"Daddy?"

"Uh, what did you say, son?"

"What's stupid?"

"Oh, nothing. Why don't you go clean your room? Daddy's

busy now."

These unguarded words from your mouth present a power-ful view of God to your children. Your seemingly casual words forcefully instruct your children about God—for good or for bad. How would Satan want you to talk to your kids about something as basic as the weather? Your big golf date (or boating day, or baseball game, or garden show, etc.) gets rained out. You find yourself angry and upset. You say something like, "Why couldn't it have waited until tomorrow? I've been weeks setting this up. Stupid rain! I can't believe what bad luck this is!"

These comments communicate to your kids just how well you think Jesus Christ, the Lord of the wind and the waves, is running His world. You are complaining against His decision to bring rain when you didn't want Him to. Whom are you pleas-ing? Whom do you think is cheering you on, saying, "Go for it, keep it up, couldn't have said it better myself, atta boy!" (Hint: it's not the Holy Spirit.)

Think about it. Do you really want to present God's actions in His world with Satan's spin? You only have so many words, so many minutes to show God's truth to your kids. God wants you to make them all count. Your children can hear Satan's spin from the world all the time. They need to hear God's truth spoken with love and awe by parents who are following God's direction in Deuteronomy 6.

The Index of Leading Cultural Indicators documents that teenagers spend only thirty-five minutes a week talking with their fathers.[1] That's five minutes each day. What do your children hear from you about God in the few minutes that you have each day to speak to them?

This concept, of course, applies to areas of life other than just the weather. The principle of Deuteronomy 6 is that your everyday comments are the ones that teach your children most profoundly about your view of God. Your interaction with God in everyday, ordinary, non-church life is the most powerful tool of influence that you have with your children. It communicates what you *really* believe. You are being either a good example of someone wholeheartedly committed to God or a bad example, depending upon how you react to everyday life. Do you see how important everyday talk is?

To make a good impression, everyday talk must be spoken with a pleasant spirit, so that children will regard your direction the same way they would a gift of fine jewelry.

You might ask, "Where did this thought come from?" Listen to Proverbs 1:8–9:

> Listen, my son, to your father's instruction
> And do not forsake your mother's teaching.
> They will be a garland to grace your head
> And a chain to adorn your neck.

Your instruction of God's Word should be given as joyfully and carefully as if you were presenting your kids with the finest jewelry to wear. Your teaching, if heeded, will make them attractive, just as fine jewelry would. Don't just throw God's Word at them. Present it with love and care.

If you bought your daughter a gold necklace for her birthday, how would you give it to her? Would you ball it up and toss it to her on her way out the door? Of course not! Would you not rather place the necklace in a jewelry box, wrap it beautifully, pick a special moment, and then give it to her? If you just balled up the necklace and threw it at her, she would probably think the necklace was on the bargain table at the dollar store. Too often, we hurl admonitions at our kids in the heat of battle, propelled by frustration and anger. Proverbs 1 encourages you to present

God's truth as the precious gift that it is. How you present it is likely to have a great influence on how children receive it. The loving presentation of God's truth is a way that you can impress God's commands on your children.

The Gospels provide the most profound illustrations of how to obey the command of Deuteronomy 6 with the power of everyday talk. Consider the example of Jesus Christ, whose everyday talk was exactly what God the Father wanted it to be—perfectly righteous and holy. In living a perfect life, He showed how to use everyday talk

Jesus used everyday talk as his primary method of teaching. In his training of the disciples, Jesus did what God instructed the Israelites to do in Deuteronomy 6. He lived Deuteronomy 6:1.[2] As a result, Jesus' disciples were different from other religious leaders. Mark 3:14 says that Jesus selected his disciples so that they might be with Him. He intentionally chose a method of teaching that involved around-the-clock discipling. They were with Him 24/7. Acts 4:13 says that it was *obvious* that the disciples had been with Jesus. There is a clear cause and effect here. He lived with them, traveled with them, ate with them, worked with them, and talked with them. In the end, they were like Him. Not perfectly, of course, but *obviously*.

How did that happen? We have the account in the Gospels. Jesus talked with His disciples about God. He used every event (and non-event) to talk to them. He used a fig tree, a sparrow, a kernel of wheat, foxes, wine, camels, gates, highways, pearls, mustard seeds, the hair on your head, money, the weather and all sorts of other things to talk to His disciples about God. This is the kind of talk Deuteronomy describes. Jesus used everyday talk to train the apostles. In the same way, God wants you to talk to your children about Him all the time. No matter what comes up during your hectic day, He wants you to talk about

Him—every day.

Does this kind of talk seem unnatural to you? We lead busy lives, and all too often lose sight of priorities. We don't take time to meditate. Talking about God isn't hard or complicated, but it does require some time and preparation. If you don't spend time *thinking* about God, you won't have much to *say* about God.

God is everywhere, all the time. He controls everything. If you are aware of His power and presence, if you take even a little time to meditate on Him, your everyday talk will begin to be about God.

Everyday talk happens; the question is, what kind do your kids get most? Following the principles just described will help you to increase your conversation time with your kids. Your teenage children need more than thirty-five minutes a week. Practicing everyday talk about God will help give you the extra time they need.

But what about the other influences on your children? You aren't the only one talking to them. Deuteronomy 6 also teaches you that children, as well as adults, are designed to be influenced by others. Jesus was with His disciples so that He could influence them. Someone will always be influencing your kids. Someone will always be using the powerful tool of everyday talk to encourage your kids either away from God or toward God. The apostle Paul knew this well when he warned the Corinthians, "Do not be deceived: 'Bad company corrupts good morals'" (I Corinthians 15:33 NASB).

You see, if you aren't talking to your kids, someone else is. The statistics indicate that teenagers are spending three hours a day watching TV. Preschoolers are watching as much as four hours per day. If teenagers are listening to three hours of TV every day and averaging five minutes a day talking with their dads, who is winning the influence battle? If your preschooler watches four hours per day, how many hours is he hearing from you about how God runs His world? It doesn't take X-rated violence, sex and language to have an ungodly influence. Even the "good" programs for children can be "bad company" if they offer an exciting, satisfying world that ignores (or denies) the sovereign God of the Bible. Do you really want your children to get the impression that it's okay to ignore God most of the time?

Paul teaches that bad company, which brings the wrong sort of everyday talk, will attack and weaken good teaching and moral character. Notice two more translations of this text:

> "Do not be misled: 'Bad company corrupts good character.'" NIV

> "Don't be misled, 'Bad companions corrupt good habits.'" CCNT

All these translations give insight into the original Greek. Bad influence (that is, bad company or companions) will act to corrupt or ruin good habits of moral character. *The Linguistic Key to the Greek New Testament* says that this corruption is active.[3] In other words, bad companions will actively attack good moral character and even overcome it if not countered. Wrong everyday talk is corrosive. It will keep on corrupting until it is stopped, cleaned up and replaced. This is something you must be concerned about. What sort of everyday talk do your children hear?

TV, videos, movies, conversations with others, listening to music—these are all sources of everyday talk. They are all influences that impact your kids along life's road. If you spend five minutes saying what is right and the influences from bad company total three hours or more, what do you think is going to have the biggest impact on your children? Your good words as a parent can be drowned out by the sheer volume of corrupting bad influences. If you don't agree, go back and read the verse again: **"Bad companions corrupt good habits."**

Everyday talk is important. Don't fall into the trap of thinking that some influences are neutral—neither good nor bad. Anything that doesn't influence your child **for God** is an influence **away from God.** Jesus taught that whoever was not with Him was against Him.

How to measure your children's everyday talk

Here is one way for you to analyze the forces influencing your child's life. Write down how your child spends his day. List how many hours he goes to school, watches TV, videos, movies, computer games, plays with friends, listens to music, sits by himself, rides the bus, etc. Evaluate whether each of the above is influencing him for good or bad. Remember that no influence is neutral. Add up the hours of good influence, and add up the hours of bad influence. Compare these totals. Add in how much time you spend influencing him for good. This will give you a picture of how much your child is being corrupted with bad company. Parent, what type of everyday talk is your child hearing most?

Do you need to begin reclaiming the influence your child receives? This is why Paul says so bluntly, "Don't be misled, [don't be fooled] bad company corrupts good character."

Now you know why everyday talk is important. You know how powerful everyday talk is. You can, in the long run, provoke your children to anger by not providing the everyday talk that God describes in Deuteronomy 6 and Ephesians 6. And you realize now that this everyday talk should be given as the most precious of gifts, because it is! Everyday talk will influence your kids either for Satan and his ways or for God and His ways. As you read this book, pray that God will use it so effectively that the everyday talk your children hear will lead them to Christ. Pray that your responses, even to something as mundane as unexpected rain, will lead to the praise of God.

Application Questions

1. What do you think your everyday talk reveals about your priorities and your worldview?

2. Make a list of twenty-five ordinary events or things that you could use for everyday talk about God.

3. When do you have everyday talk with your children?

4. What opportunities do you have to increase or improve your everyday talk?

Footnotes

[1] William J. Bennett, *The Index of Leading Cultural Indicators: Facts and Figures on the State of American Society.* (New York: Simon and Schuster, 1994) 102-103

[2] Jesus' "everyday talk" was not unplanned or unthinking, of course, as ours often is.

[3] Fritz Reinecker and Cleon Rogers, *Linguistic Key to the Greek New Testament* (Grand Rapids: Zondervan Publishing Co., 1980) , p. 443.

Your Children and the Gospel

Your child began life as an enemy of God.

He (or she) was an unregenerate, sinful, rebellious enemy of God.

Do you believe this?

If you do, you can have great hope and peace about your child and his relationship to God. If you don't believe this, then you will have no reason to tell your child what he needs to know to become God's friend.

Paul teaches in Romans that all have sinned and come short of God's glory (Romans 3:23) and that there isn't anybody who is righteous, not a single one (Romans 3:10). This is also what David says in Psalm 51:5, "Surely I was sinful at birth, sinful from the time my mother conceived me."

Paul sums this doctrine up in Ephesians 2:1–3:

> And you were dead in your trespasses and sins, in which
> you formerly walked according to the course of this
> world, according to the prince of the power of the air, of

the spirit that is now working in the sons of disobedience.
Among them we too all formerly lived in the lusts of our
flesh, indulging the desires of the flesh and of the mind,
and were by nature children of wrath, even as the rest
(NASB).

The Bible is clear: your child, as well as you, was born an
enemy of God and fully deserving of His wrath. This is not
a popular thought today. More often, people see children as
innocent victims. If they do something wrong, it is probably
just because they haven't learned better yet (after all, they're just
children), or they have had negative role models.

The Bible's negative statements about human nature may
seem harsh and offensive, but they are true. In this case, the hard
truth is the kindest message. The Bible explains the problem
accurately, and then it also gives you the right answer to that
problem. The answer of hope is that those who are born the
enemies of God can know peace with God through the gospel
of Jesus Christ.

Before I discuss how to present the gospel to young children,
let me mention another mistaken view of children. Sometimes
parents take seriously the biblical doctrine of sin, but then lose
their balance in the other direction. They know their children
are born with wicked, sinful hearts, and so they are pessimis-
tic about their young children's ability to understand the gospel.
They tend to be doubtful about the sincerity of a young child's
prayer or profession of faith. They take a "wait and see" attitude,
carefully scrutinizing the child's behavior to judge whether he
produces consistent spiritual fruit. Sometimes parents require
more spiritual fruit from professing children than they do from
professing adults. But the gospel message, properly understood,
deals with both of these wrong views: insisting that children are

basically good, and imposing a false standard of performance on children.

What is the Gospel?

I Corinthians 15:3–4 says it consists of three parts: " . . . for I delivered to you as of first importance what I also received, that Christ died for our sins according to the Scriptures, and that He was buried, and that He was raised on the third day according to the Scriptures" (NASB).

The first element is that Christ died for our sins according to the Scriptures. The Scriptures teach that man is hopelessly guilty before God from the moment of birth. God is a holy God who demands perfection. Christ is the only One who can satisfy God's requirements for a perfect life. Therefore, Christian, when Christ died for your sins, God was satisfied.

The second element is that by dying Christ actually paid the full penalty for our sins. Christ, the man, died so that you and all men who trust in Him could live.

The third element is that Christ conquered death when He was raised from the dead as God promised. This gospel message is found throughout the whole Bible beginning with Genesis 3:15.

This is the good news. It is not complicated. It is centered on the work of Christ, not man. Only Christ can satisfy God's demand for justice and perfection. God only requires that you and your children believe this by faith in order to know Him. He even provides this faith as a gift because we cannot produce faith in ourselves (Ephesians 2:1–8).

THE GOSPEL

- Jesus died for our sins as the Scriptures teach.

- The wrath of God that we deserved was turned fully and awfully upon Jesus. Therefore He died and was buried.

- Jesus rose from the dead, defeating the power of sin and Satan, and gives new life to His own.

This is the gospel. This is what the Bible teaches about the gospel. This message of good news brings life and light to a dark world. This same message will bring life and light to your child.

What do your children think the gospel is?

Do your children believe the gospel of Christ is about His performance on the cross? Or do your kids think that the gospel means God will only be pleased if they obey him and obey you? Do your kids think that the gospel means that they must be good so God will love them? Do your kids think that they must be good for *you* to like them, for *you* to love them? Your everyday talk teaches your functional understanding of the gospel to your children. Does your everyday talk center upon grace or performance?

Listen to your children talk about their understanding of the gospel. They do, you know. You may be thinking that children seldom, if ever, sit around and talk about the gospel. Actually, they do all the time. Listen to your children talk. Listen to what makes them happy or sad. Listen to what they say about how you love them. Listen, listen, listen.

"Mommy, I'm sorry I make you angry."

"Daddy, I won't do it again."

"Why is everybody mad at me?"

"Do you think God is mad at me?"

"He hurt me, so I hit him back."

"I am sorry that I am not good enough to make you happy."

"I'll be good, I promise. Please don't be mad at me."

"I try and try and try but I just can't do what you want me to."

"I guess I am just not good enough."

"Mommy, I just can't do it. I try but I just can't."

Have you ever heard words like these from your children? These statements indicate what your children think about the gospel. These kinds of statements show that performance (not grace) forms the basis of how your children are attempting to relate to you and to God.

Are you able to delight in your children simply because God gave them to you and you love them? Or must your children behave in a way that pleases you before you can delight in them?

The purpose of this book is to help you, parent, to reflect the power of gospel grace in your everyday talk. As this powerful grace begins to control your everyday talk, you will lead your children to a rich and growing understanding of the gospel. When your children complain that they can't do what God wants, you will seize the opportunity to respond with the powerful gospel of grace. This is your opportunity to say, "Sweetheart, I know that you can't obey by yourself. This is why Jesus died. He did what you cannot do. Now He can help you to trust Him. Let's ask Jesus to forgive you and help you love Him by the power of His gospel."

Teach your children to pray and ask for God's forgiveness and God's strength to obey Him.

Teach your children to pray and ask God to help them love Him. Teach your children that God delights in their prayers when they repent and ask for His help. Jesus taught His disciples how to pray and what to pray for. God also instructs you to teach your children how to pray and what to pray for. This is Paul's point in Ephesians 6:4 when he directs fathers to raise their children in "the fear and admonition of the Lord."

Here is an example of how you can lead your children to the power of the gospel. For the purpose of this discussion we will look only at Sarah's response, although Brandon also needs attention.

You hear a loud cry coming from the children's room. You walk into the room and discover that Sarah, your four-year-old daughter, has just hit Brandon, your three-year-old son, because he wouldn't give her the toy she wanted. You take Sarah into your room and administer the appropriate discipline. Sarah sadly tells you she knows that she should not have hit Brandon, but she just was so angry with him that she did it anyway. She tells you that she just can't do it, she can't obey and be good.

What do you say as a parent?

Response # 1 —*Mom replies with an even but stern voice,* "Well, Sarah, that is what discipline is for. Eventually, you will learn that it is wrong to hit when you're angry. If Mommy disciplines you enough times you will get the message. Please don't hit Brandon any more. We don't solve problems by hitting."

Response # 2 —*Mom replies with a tone of exasperation.* "I know Sarah, you always say that. But, you just have to learn to be good. How many times must mommy spank you? You shouldn't do something you know is wrong. Maybe someday you will change."

Response # 3 —*Mom replies in anger,* "Sarah, if you wanted to be good and stop hitting Brandon, you would. Mommy is really losing patience with you. Your father and I are going to have a long talk when he gets home. This has got to stop. This is the fourth time this week."

Response # 4 —*Mom responds in dejected frustration,* "Sarah, I don't know what to do with you. Mommy has tried and tried to teach you what is right. I just don't know what to do. I can't seem to make you change. I just don't know what to do."

All of these responses are performance-based. They result in broken relationships, not healthy ones. Mom is treating Sarah as if she could solve her problem with sin by responding in her own strength, simply by doing what Mommy says. "Just do it," she says, in effect. The problem is that Sarah, like everyone else on planet Earth, can't do good in her own strength. All of these first four responses might produce a fine Pharisee, but they will not lead to new life in Christ for your child.

Contrast the first four responses with this next one.

Response # 5 —*Mom replies with warmth and understanding,* "Sarah, I know you can't obey by yourself. I know that. But that is why Jesus died on the cross, because we can't do it ourselves. Remember the Bible says that Jesus died so that we would have new life. You can't obey in your own strength, but you can obey in Jesus' strength. Let's pray right now and ask Jesus to help."

"Dear God, please help me to obey you and love you. I just can't do it by myself. Please forgive me for hitting Brandon. Please help me to trust you. I know that you are the only one who can help me be different and turn my heart to you. Please help me to obey Mommy and to obey you. In Jesus' name, Amen."

This simple little prayer addresses the issues at hand. Sarah needs Jesus to help her to obey. Sarah acknowledges that she must change. She turns to Christ for help.

At this point I can imagine someone thinking, "What four-year-old child is going to come up with that prayer? Are you kidding me?!?"

Your four-year-old can "come up with this prayer" the same way the disciples came up with the Lord's Prayer. You teach it to her, just as Jesus taught the Lord's Prayer to the disciples. Luke 11 records that Jesus taught His disciples His prayer word for word. This is how you start with your children. Help them pray by teaching them word for word what to say to God. Teach your children to pray phrase by phrase, by repeating each phrase after you say it. Jesus didn't wait for His disciples to become spiritual enough to know what to pray and how to pray. He told them what to say and how to pray, word for word. Spirituality doesn't come by waiting for it to appear. Spirituality comes by teaching what the Holy Spirit has written at the time it is needed. When the disciples asked Jesus to teach them how to pray, He taught them word for word—in the middle of their everyday lives. Jesus taught his disciples everyday prayer.

As a parent you must exercise patience as you pray this prayer and others like it over and over again with your children. By doing this you are teaching your children that you can't be a good parent in your own strength either. As your children repeat this prayer, you also pray that God would honor His word and hear the plea of this child who is in deep need of God's love and mercy and power to obey. After they learn to follow the pattern of prayer you provide, they will eventually begin to formulate their own prayers, following that example. This is the power of the gospel. It is the greatest gift that you can give to your child.

Application Questions

1. How can you use your child's disobedience to lead him to (or remind him of) the gospel?

2. How can you lead your child to obedience by explaining the gospel?

3. How would you explain the importance of prayer in obedience?

4. What is the difference between punishment and discipline?

Listening to Your Children

Good everyday talk requires at least two components. One is that you must have good things to say. The other component is good listening. In this chapter we will focus on listening. You must be a good listener before you can say helpful things to your children.

It is hard to be a good listener.

It is much easier to speak first, thinking you will listen later. But often, speaking first means losing the opportunity to listen at all.

Let me repeat, it is hard to be a good listener. The pressing issues of everyday life are obstacles to good, everyday listening. You can become so focused on your own problems that you fail to be a good listener. This sort of preoccupation leads to what I call *parentspeak*. *Parentspeak* is talking without listening. This is the sort of everyday talk that damages your relationship with your kids. Most parents do this at times, sometimes without even being conscious of it. Here is an example of *parentspeak*. See if this conversation sounds at all familiar to you.

You have just gotten home from work. Your son finds you molded into your favorite chair, reading your paper or the mail as you start to unwind.

"Dad?"

"Huh?"

"Dad?"

"Yeah, readinpapernow."

"Dad?"

"Uh, um, speakintome?"

"Dad?"

"Uh, justaminute."

"Dad?"

"Didyaaskyormother?"

"Dad?"

"Notnow,jusgothome. gottarelax, OK?"

"Dad?"

"Umdiyousaysomthin? uhwhatimeisgameon?"

"Dad?"

"Beforyoustart, didyoufinishyourschoolstuff?"

As your son turns to leave, you call after him and say, "Sonisanythingwrong?"

Your son says, "Nothing's wrong. Bye, Dad." You shake your head and go back to your paper.

This is not the sort of everyday talk that will be helpful to your kids.

Sometimes your son might actually get to say more than just, "Dad." He might even get a whole sentence out before *parentspeak* takes over.

"Hey, Dad, you know that slippery hill in the jungle over at Jared's house?"

In absent-minded exasperation, you say, "Hill? What hill?

Jared who? Can this wait? I'm busy reading right now. You know we don't have hills or jungles around here."

Your son turns and walks away.

I picked on dads in this illustration, but moms can be just as guilty of *parentspeak*. *Parentspeak* is talking without listening. Your words may not run together as in the first example, but anytime you speak without listening—really listening—you engage in *parentspeak*. You may think you have good reasons for not listening. You are tired. You have important business decisions to consider. There may be a problem in your marriage relationship. You are trying to think how you will get all the yard work or housework done. You might be worried about bills. You desperately need to relax. Or maybe you are just preoccupied. You don't want to ignore your children—you are just thinking about other things. However, if your words are going to please God and benefit your children, you must first be a good listener.

Did I say that good listening is hard? It is. It requires sacrificial love and self-denial to give your child the time and attention to listen closely.

Consider *parentspeak* for a moment. Do you use it? Does it creep into your everyday talk? Does it, perhaps, dominate your everyday talk? As you reflect on your own speech patterns, don't look only for the absentminded mumbling of the previous example. *Parentspeak* can take other forms as well. It can be clear and direct language. *Parentspeak* may also sound like this: "Sarah, tonight, before you go to bed, I want you to finish cleaning your room, do the dishes, finish your homework, write your grandmother and don't listen to any music until all that is finished. Is that clear?"

You may be protesting, "What is wrong with this? Clear, directive speech is necessary for running a good household!"

I agree. But still, it may qualify as *parentspeak*. If this type of speaking forms the majority of your communication with your children, then it is *parentspeak*. Recall our working definition for *parentspeak*. *Parentspeak* is talking without listening. What does the Bible say about this type of speaking?

> "He who answers before listening—that is his folly and
> his shame" (Proverbs 18:13).

Before you can answer your children, before you can say things that are helpful, you must first listen. It is hard to be a good listener. But Proverbs 18:13 says *parentspeak* is a shame to you. *Parentspeak* is the opposite of good listening and, therefore, the enemy of good, productive, everyday talk. But be encouraged! Proverbs 18:15 has the cure for *parentspeak*.

> "The heart of the discerning acquires knowledge; the ears
> of the wise seek it out."

God wants you to have active ears. That is why listening is hard. We aren't accustomed to listening aggressively. We tend to have active mouths, but not active ears. If your ears seek out knowledge about your children, they can provide you with the knowledge you need for productive, everyday talk with your kids. This is what Proverbs 18:15 is teaching you. As you and your children walk, run, drive and sometimes stumble along the road of life that Deuteronomy 6 talks about, your ears should be in "seek mode." It is difficult to listen and talk at the same time. If you want better communication with your children, you must have ears that seek out knowledge about them. Are you actively listening to your children? Do you ever take time just to sit in the next room and listen to them when they are not aware you are listening?

This might seem impossible, or at best impractical. However, think with me for a moment about situations when you do have active ears. Do you listen to your boss or supervisor at work? Are you eager to catch a word or a phrase that might pertain to you or your job? If your supervisor walks by and makes a comment in passing, do you ignore it? If your supervisor says your name, do you ignore it? Do you think, "If he really wants to talk with me, he'll try again when I am not so busy?" No, of course not! Your ears are in seek mode, listening for any tidbit or word fragment that might impact you. A supervisor can whisper your name from across the room, and you come running. Seemingly through closed doors, you can hear a phrase that was spoken about you. You have active ears whenever you want to.

With regard to your children, God wants you to have active ears, ears that seek out knowledge. God wants you to listen to your children. Listen for the things that they don't say as well as what they do say. Become a parent with active ears.

Let's look again at the jungle at Jared's house. The difference this time is that the father has been following Proverbs 18:15. His ears have been active. Listen to the difference.

"Hey, Dad, you know that slippery hill in the jungle over at Jared's house?"

"Let me think, Ethan. Oh! You mean over at the new kid's house where he has that really neat backyard that looks just like a jungle? The place where you thought you might see some dangerous jungle creatures?"

"Yeah, Dad, that's the place. Well, let me ask you something about what Jared did . . .."

Why the big difference this time? Dad had active ears. He remembered that Jared was a son of the new family in the neighborhood, and that he got along well with Ethan. Even though Dad knew that Jared's hill was actually a little mound of dirt behind some shrubs, he also knew that to a seven-year-old boy, this made a great jungle.

This time, Dad knew what Ethan was talking about. So, Ethan asked Dad a question. This is your goal. You want your children to ask you questions. According to Deuteronomy 6:20, your child's questions provide teaching opportunities.

"In the future, when your son asks you, 'What is the meaning of the stipulations, decrees and laws the LORD our God has commanded you?' . . . " (NIV). Don't be put off by the language of stipulations, decrees and laws. Moses is simply saying that when your son asks you about how God's law works, that's your cue to tell him about God's faithfulness. The passage in Deuteronomy 6:4–9 assumes that the result of impressing the truth of God upon the hearts of your children is that they will ask you questions about where they are on life's path.

Your children can never ask you too many questions.

This may seem like lunacy, especially if you have a two- or three-year-old child, but it's true. You want them to ask you questions. If you teach them that God controls the world, and if you teach them that everything that happens to them is planned by God so that they would look to Him, then your children will ask you questions about what God is doing with His world. They will ask you about what God is doing along the pathway of their lives. This is your goal—to have your children ask you about what God is doing in their lives.

Your progress as a parent can be measured by the questions your kids ask. You will always hear mundane questions such as, "What's for supper?" or, "May I borrow the keys?" However, you also want to hear questions like these:

"Mom, why was Sonya saying words that are bad? Why

was she mad at me?"

"Dad, why can't I have as much fun all the time as I do at Jared's house?"

"Mom, why did that dog have to jump out and eat that little rabbit?"

"Mom, why don't I fit in with everybody else? Is something wrong with me?"

"Dad, why is it that sometimes I want to use bad language the way some of the other kids do?"

These questions will not come unless you are a good listener, a Proverbs 18:15 listener. In a later chapter we will talk about Ephesians 4:29, which deals even more powerfully with good listening. For now, take a moment to evaluate with your husband or wife how much of your conversation with your children is *parentspeak* and how much is genuine listening.

This is how you are able to have everyday talk that helps. It does not come easily. It requires faith, time and love. Do you know what your child thinks about where he has been? God wants you to listen carefully. And as you care for your kids they will want you to know their thoughts, and they will tell you.

The better you know your children, the more you can shine the powerful light of Scripture into the dark corners of their lives. Your words can confront them with the heart-changing power of His Word. God wants your words to flow from a discerning, understanding heart. God wants you to be a good listener.

Application Questions

1. Do you recognize any ways in which you practice *parent-speak*? If so, list how and when.

2. Building on your answer to the first question, what would you say instead of *parentspeak* at your next opportunity? Write out actual responses.

3. In your conversations with your children, what is the percentage of time you listen? What is the percentage of time you talk?

4. Do you know of any issues your child wants to discuss with you—but you haven't had time yet?

Four

Holy Directions!

No, this is not the opening line of a new batman movie. This chapter is about giving directions to your children. Giving directions to your children is an important part of everyday talk. You should give holy directions. Remember, to be holy means to be different, set apart for a special purpose. It simply means that the directions you give as a Christian parent will be unlike the directions a non-Christian parent gives.

Giving directions assumes authority.

If you don't have authority, why should anyone follow your orders? But that raises this question: who made you the boss? Why do you have authority over your children? Simply put—because God says so.

The illustration below shows that God has established you as the authority over your children, but that your children are accountable first of all to God for their actions. This is what Ephesians 6:1–4 is teaching:

Children, obey your parents in the Lord, for this is
right. **Honor your father and mother** (which is the
first commandment with a promise), **so that it may be
well with you, and that you may live long on the earth.**
Fathers, do not provoke your children to anger, but bring
them up in the discipline and instruction of the Lord
(NASB).

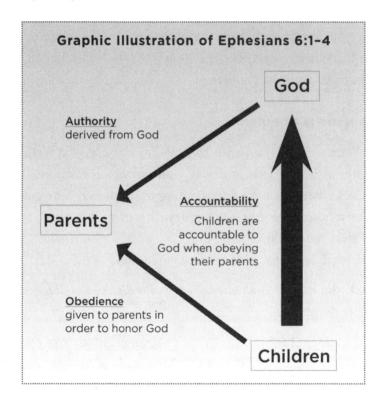

Children are commanded to obey their parents in the Lord.
God is the one who establishes the authority of the parent and
determines what they must teach. The children will be blessed if
they obey. It is not the parents who have the ability to bless with
long life, but God. Therefore, children are ultimately accountable to God.

To make this practical, let's move right to your everyday world. There is perhaps no more ordinary, everyday, unglamorous task than taking out the garbage. You probably did it as a child, and now, as a parent, you have the right to pass this duty along to your children. You want the garbage taken out. It's a daily necessity of life. The garbage must be taken out.

The issue is simple, yet often there is a battle over the garbage. You announce that you want the garbage taken out. Two hours later you return and there the garbage sits. The stage is set. The battle is engaged. The question is, "Who will take out the garbage, you or your children?"

The issue is obedience.

Your view of obedience controls how you give directions. Strange as it may seem, the way your garbage is taken out can reveal your functional understanding of obedience. The goal is to learn how to give holy, everyday directions that please God and bless your children.

Let me begin by asking you two questions:

Do you want your children to obey your directions and take out the garbage?

You might be thinking, "That's a strange question; of course I want my children to obey me." That leads me to the second question.

Assuming you want your children to obey you, do you act as if you expect them to take out the garbage?

Now you are sure I am asking stupid questions. "What do you mean, do I act like I want them to take it out? Of course I do!"

Okay, let's examine some ways that parents typically ask for obedience. In this illustration, Joshua is eight years old. How many ways can Mom ask Josh to take out the garbage?

"Joshua, if you want to be helpful, you could take out the garbage sometime when you have some free time." Or,

"Josh, take out the garbage right now!!"

"Joshua, I asked you yesterday and the day before and the day before that, would you please find time to take out the garbage!"

"Joshua, please think of things to do to help out, like maybe take out the garbage. Okay?"

"Mommy is sooo tired of taking out the garbage all the time. Josh, wouldn't you like to help me?"

"Joshua, take out the garbage right now, or I will take away your TV privileges for three days!"

"When I was your age, I always had to take out the garbage every day, whether I wanted to or not. Now take out the garbage!"

"Joshua, this is it! I am not going to ask you again. Take out the garbage!"

"Joshua, if you do not take out the garbage this instant, you are going to get the biggest spanking of your life, and you will get it when your father gets home."

None of these directives to Joshua fit the biblical concept of obedience. Yes, some of the instructions were direct, but many were not. Each reflects a parent who does not really expect to be obeyed. All of these attempts at securing obedience from Joshua fall into the category of manipulation and bargaining. You want the garbage taken out. Joshua does not want to take it out. You cajole, order, plead, bargain, in short, do anything you can to get Joshua to take the garbage out. After awhile you may even give up and take the garbage out yourself, just to end the unpleasantness and frustration.

God does not want your children to obey you simply because you are bigger than they are and can physically control them. Obedience is more than giving in to coaxing or threats. God wants your children to obey you because it pleases Him and blesses them. How can you tell the difference? Here is the request from a parent who expects Joshua to take out the garbage.

"Joshua, take the garbage out now, please."

"Sure, Mom, no problem."

Here, Joshua's mom expects to be obeyed. She doesn't ask Joshua a question, she gives him clear, pleasant direction. She doesn't whine or plead or bargain or threaten. She speaks directly but pleasantly. Joshua knows exactly what she wants him to do and when. Joshua has been trained to understand that obeying Mom is doing exactly what he is told, right away, with a good attitude.

Joshua's response is not one that came naturally to him. He is not just a "good kid." He had to be taught. His parents trained him to respond this way. When he was younger, Josh's parents taught him that he must obey his parents because the Bible says, "Children, obey your parents in the Lord, for this is right" (Eph. 6:1). They taught him that obeying his parents was obeying God.

Joshua was taught that when he is given a command by his parents, the response that pleases God is a pleasant affirmative. He learned Philippians 2:14, "Do everything without complaining or arguing, ..." So, Josh was taught to answer a command with "Sure, Mom, I'd be happy to," or something similar.

The results speak for themselves. A child who obeys promptly and pleasantly is a pleasure to be around. No one argues with that. But the big question is—how? How do I teach my child to obey like that?

Godly obedience begins with teaching children a basic worldview.

"Worldview" might sound too complicated for children, but it's really not. It's as simple as saying, "God made everything. He made you. God is in charge of everything and we must obey Him." That's just the beginning, but, at a child's level, it is the basis for obedience.

Josh's parents used Proverbs 16:20-24 to impress on Josh one of the most basic components of a Christian worldview. Verse 22 is the center and anchor of this passage.

> Understanding is a fountain of life to those who have it,
> but folly brings punishment to fools. (Proverbs 16:22)

Biblical wisdom brings life. Following God's ways brings life. This is the enormous benefit of obedience. Josh learned early that only Christ could give him the strength to obey with a joyful heart. When Joshua was learning to trust God this way, there were many rocky moments. However, discipline was lovingly applied and Joshua was encouraged with pleasant, not harsh, instruction.

So now, at age eight, Joshua responds with something like, "Sure, I'd be happy to, no problem," when he is given a command or directive. When he doesn't, he is lovingly and firmly disciplined by his parents. But even when that has to happen, his underlying attitude is based on the God-given knowledge that "understanding is a fountain of life to those who have it." He is not a "perfect little angel." He is still an active, rowdy, eight-year-old boy. But even a child can possess genuine biblical wisdom and insight when he has been taught God's ways consistently, and when he has learned through obedience,

Let's look carefully at the verses that surround Proverbs 16:22 to learn what God has in mind. This passage teaches not only the value of possessing godly wisdom, but also the best approach to teaching it.

> Whoever gives heed to instruction prospers, and blessed is he who trusts in the LORD. The wise in heart are called discerning, and pleasant words promote instruction. Understanding is a fountain of life to those who have it, but folly brings punishment to fools. A wise man's heart guides his mouth, and his lips promote instruction. Pleasant words are a honeycomb, sweet to the soul and healing to the bones. (Proverbs 16:20–24)

In interpreting this passage, we must realize that *Proverbs* is part of a particular literary genre. It is Hebrew poetry, part of biblical "wisdom literature." The Hebrew appears to indicate that these five verses have the following poetic structure[1]:

He who follows instruction will do well (20)

Sweet words increase the likelihood that instruction will be received. (21)

God's wisdom brings life, but the instruction of fools brings destruction. (22)

The heart of the wise will guide his speech and make his speech persuasive. (23)

Kind, pleasant words bring sweet healing to the soul and body of the listener. (24)

This set of five verses forms a chiasm, a concentric parallelism. They form a unit of thought concerning the role of pleasant words and obedience. The climax or heart of the section is at the center, in verse 22. Parents, you will benefit from the truth and the power of the words if you take time to think about them. Don't miss this. The verses show you how to give holy directions. You do not need any statistics to tell you that communication with children, especially teenage children, can be difficult and painful. Let this passage help you learn to use pleasant, healing words to build patterns of obedience now that will serve you, your children and God in the years ahead.

Look again at the structure of the five verses, with verse 22 at the center. It is the core concept of the passage. This verse states God's goal for your instruction. Understanding biblical wisdom brings life. *This is why you want Joshua to obey.* Following God's ways brings life. If Joshua follows the lead of those who do not love God, he will destroy his life.

What is the "life" that biblical wisdom brings? This is spiritual life, which only Christians possess; all others are spiritually dead. Christians who faithfully practice living in God's ways acquire wisdom, and they experience greater spiritual blessings than those who stumble along, foolishly ignoring His instructions.

Please don't misunderstand. I am not saying that obedience brings new life in Christ. Neither is Proverbs 16:22 saying this. True obedience to God's commands is the result, the fruit, of a life given over to God. Not following God's direction is destructive.

Parent, you have had this lesson demonstrated to you countless times in contexts other than child rearing. What happens when you respond angrily because you think your spouse has been unkind to you? You don't respond in God's way, with a soft answer, but you snap back, returning evil for evil. What is the impact? Things get worse, don't they? That's right. For the moment there is a destructive impact on your relationship. The same is true for your children and obedience. If God is obeyed, life is pursued. So the goal for your children is for them to embrace God's ways, which bring life.

This is what makes the task of Joshua's taking out the garbage one of spiritual significance. Your ultimate goal is not to get the garbage out of the house for your own convenience. Your goal is to have your child know God and happily serve Him. This is why bargaining, cajoling, pleading and similar ploys are so damaging

Remember, the basic issue in obedience is willing submission. Unwilling, grudging compliance is not godly obedience. Cooperation based on negotiation and mutual advantage is also not obedience. Biblical obedience is willing submission to authority.

Let's look again at the requests to take out the garbage, with an analysis of each response.

1.   *"Joshua, if you want to be helpful, you could take out the garbage sometime when you have some free time."*

While this request may sound pleasant and considerate, it contains some serious problems. Children need to be instructed (see Proverbs 1:8-9; Eph.6:1-3). Asking Joshua if he wants to be helpful removes this request from the realm of instruction. What he wants is not the issue. Also, the directive is not specific as to timing. Joshua can do it whenever he thinks he has free time. This will encourage Joshua to think that the issues of helping and free time are his to decide. This is not good for an eight-year-old. Many adults struggle with these issues. Certainly, Josh still needs direction. Here, the initiative is left with Joshua instead of his parents. This request allows Joshua to decide that he won't have free time for several hours or even days, leaving a problem of overflowing garbage bags, a selfish child and a frustrated parent.

2. *"Josh, take out the garbage right now!!"*

A sharp command will stir up anger and not promote understanding or obedience, just a grudging compliance.

3. *"Joshua, I asked you yesterday and the day before and the day before that. Would you please find time to take out the garbage!"*

This request begs the question of who is responsible. The parent is the one to blame here because she has not seen to it that that she was obeyed the first time. Note again that the parent, not Joshua, is the one who should decide Joshua's time priorities.

4. *"Joshua, please think of things to do to help out, like maybe take out the garbage. Okay?"*

This is a formula for producing a whining spirit in your children. This parent is whining to her child. Joshua will likely follow the example and whine himself. This non-directive request allows the child to ignore the garbage without technically disobeying. Giving Joshua clear, precise instructions is the best way to help him think of things to do to help.

5. *"Mommy is sooo tired of taking out the garbage all the time. Josh, wouldn't you like to help me?"*

Again, this is Mommy's problem. This form of manipulation is trying to get Joshua to have sympathy for Mom and take out the garbage for her so she won't be tired. When Joshua doesn't take out the garbage, three bad things happen. The garbage piles up. Joshua ignores Mom without consequences. Joshua's mother feels hurt because she thinks Joshua doesn't care that she is tired.

6.   *"Joshua, take out the garbage right now, or I will take away your TV privileges for three days!"*

This really amounts to a manipulative threat. Joshua is pretty sure that he won't lose TV for three hours, let alone three days. This command also illustrates that the parent does not expect her command to be obeyed. If obedience were expected, then "Take out the garbage now," would be sufficient.

7.   *"When I was your age, I always had to take out the garbage, whether I wanted to or not. Now take out the garbage."*

Adding extra issues from your childhood will not motivate your child to obey more quickly. This is another example of a parent who is frustrated with a lack of quick, consistent, pleasant obedience from her child.

8.   *"Joshua, I am not going to ask you again. Take out the garbage!"*

Both the parent and Joshua know that she will ask again.

9.   *"Joshua, if you do not take out the garbage this instant, you are going to get the biggest spanking of your life—when your father gets home."*

This is yet another example of a frustrated mom who knows that her child is not obeying. The extra threat doesn't really address the main issue of a child who obeys only when he really has to and certainly not at the first request. Joshua knows he probably won't get the spanking.

Perhaps you have been able to identify with one of the above examples. What needs to change? How do you apply Proverbs 16:22?

"Understanding is a fountain of life to those who have it, but folly brings punishment to fools."

You want your child to enjoy the fountain of life, not suffer the punishment of fools. This should motivate all of your instruction to your children. The other verses in this chiasm of Proverbs 16:20–24 show how this is accomplished.

Look at the parallel thoughts of verses 20 and 24. The content of the two verses is not identical; one builds on the other.

> Whoever gives heed to instruction prospers,
> and blessed is he who trusts in the LORD.

> Pleasant words are a honeycomb,
> sweet to the soul and healing to the bones.

Verse 20 underscores what you have just been looking at; obeying God's instruction is a good thing. Verse 24 addresses how this instruction should be delivered. If you want your child to know God's blessing, speak with pleasant words. Honey was the sweetest substance known to the Hebrews of Solomon's day, when the Proverbs were written. Verse 24 forms a vivid word picture for you. Pleasant words result in healing and pleasure.[2] Pleasant words are healing words that have a direct spiritual and physical impact.

Your own experience confirms this. How do you feel when

your boss speaks harshly to you at work? Both your spirit and your body are profoundly affected. The same is true with your children. Remember, the goal of your instruction is not only to have the garbage taken out, but also, primarily, to teach your children the joy of obeying God.

Proverbs 16:20 and 24 support the theme of verse 22: understanding leads to life. You want your instruction to lead to that life-giving understanding. Therefore, you will use pleasant words to promote your instruction.

Now look at the next set of verses, 21 and 23.

> The wise in heart are called discerning,
> and pleasant words promote instruction.
>
> A wise man's heart guides his mouth,
> and his lips promote instruction.

These two verses support verse 22 by stressing *what* promotes instruction. A wise man, or wise parent, will be promoting instruction so that God will be known. Verse 21 is profoundly clear and makes the point that pleasant words promote instruction.[3] This truth is so simply stated that its power may be lost. Pleasant words promote instruction! Think about the last confrontation that you had with your children about obedience. Was the problem that you spoke pleasantly, clearly, specifically to your children? Or was the problem that there was frustration, anger and harsh language from both you and your children? Listen to God again: "Pleasant words promote instruction."

What is your everyday talk like with regard to obedience? Are your directives delivered in pleasant words? Perhaps you think that things are so bad that pleasant words will not work. That is not what God says. He says that pleasant words promote instruction. James restates this in the first chapter of his letter, " . . . but everyone must be quick to hear, slow to speak and slow to anger; for the anger of man does not achieve the righteousness of God" (James 1:19-20).

Your anger will not get the job done. Go back and reread the section earlier in this chapter concerning how Joshua was properly taught about obedience.

There is much more that could be said here. But I want to close this chapter with one thought ringing in your mind. **Pleasant words promote instruction.** Is this the everyday experience you have with your children in giving them instruction? Are pleasant words a primary tool that you use in your everyday talk to accomplish God's purposes?

Meditate on these five verses in Proverbs 16. Before God, you want your children to remember that you used pleasant words to bring home the power of His truth. If you have failed in this area, don't despair. God will help you to begin using pleasant words to promote His instruction. You can give holy directions!

Application Questions

1. How many times should you repeat a command to your child before he obeys? How many times, in actual practice, do you usually repeat a command?

2. What are some excuses you might be tempted to make for your child's disobedience? How should you deal with those issues?

3. In what kinds of situations do you find it most difficult to use pleasant words to promote instruction?

4.   What is the effect on your children when you use "unpleas-
     ant," angry words? What is the effect on you?

Footnotes

[1] I owe this insight to Mark Futato, Professor of Old Testament at Reformed
Theological Seminary, Orlando, who suggested to me that these verses
might form a chiasm.

[2] Also, Proverbs 15:1 says a harsh word stirs up anger and, thus, is not pleasant or healing.

[3] The rod also promotes instruction; Proverbs 13:24; etc. The rod is to be
used in conjunction with pleasant words. Too often parents abandon
God's order. They discipline after speaking harshly has failed. Much
energy is spent in anger and harsh words. Use of the rod in this context
will only lead to more relational breakdown and is not biblical. Rather,
use of the rod is designed to be used in the context of pleasant words as
Proverbs 16 indicates.

Five

Don't Be Ordinary

In the last chapter we talked about giving directions. In this chapter we will discuss how to talk to your children when they disobey your directions. They will, you know. No matter how pleasantly your words promote instruction, your children are still sinners! They will be stubborn, deceitful, manipulative and rebellious. They will complain, whine and grumble. Your job is to recognize their sin for what it is and teach them how to deal with it God's way.

Your job is not easy. The close and constant relationship you have with your children requires constant sacrifice and self-denial. The temptations to exasperation, anger and impatience are frequent, if not constant. Parents can easily fall into the pattern of shrugging off their own sinful behavior with excuses of long days, sleepless nights and ordinary human limits.

"I'm only human. I can only take so much!" protests a weary young mom. That's a good point. How much can you take? After all, just think about how young children treat their parents.

How do you respond to people who deliberately sin against you?

How do you talk to someone who is angry at you when you have only been trying to help? What do you think of someone who hurts you deeply? If given the choice, do you try to avoid these kinds of people?

How do you talk to people who sin against you?

This is a question that parents must face head on. These people are your own children. Your Bible teaches you that your children are born in sin and will not naturally do what is right, but what is wrong. Your children will follow the desires of their own flesh. Meditate for a moment on the two passages below:

> Surely I was sinful at birth, sinful from the time my mother conceived me. (Psalm 51:5)

> As it is written: 'There is no one righteous, not even one; there is no one who understands, no one who seeks God. All have turned away, they have together become worthless; there is no one who does good, not even one.' (Rom 3:10–12)

These passages describe your children at birth. Your children need the cleansing blood of Christ to be different from what these passages describe them to be. Your children need the training and counsel of the Word of God to be anything other than Satan's ally. A direct implication of these verses for you is that your children will say and do things that hurt you. Your own children will sin against you.

How will you respond to this sin? Specifically, how will your children's sin affect your everyday talk?

How do you respond when your children treat you unfairly,

when they are disrespectful to you, or when they seem to forget all you have done for them? Your young child may have just told his first lie to you. Your older child may have hidden the fact that he broke a piece of fine crystal and then, having been discovered, seems not to care. Your teenager is mad at you for not allowing her to go to a party that *everybody* is going to. What thoughts race to your mind? How does this come out in your everyday talk?

The passages in Psalm 51 and Romans 3 teach that your children will sin against you. So you should not be surprised at their sin. It is a given. The only real question is how to respond by pleasing God and helping your children when they sin against you.

What is your typical, habitual response when you are hurt by someone? Do you just "get over it" and move on? Do you get mad? Do you struggle with anger or self pity? Do you tend to withdraw? Do you give up and think, "What's the use of trying?" Perhaps you experience a mixture of all of the above. If so, you are not alone. Most people can identify with you. However, these ordinary responses are wrong. God does not want you to be an ordinary parent.

God wants you to be a holy parent, even when you are hurting.

He has given you loving instruction in His Word on how to be the parent He wants you to be. Remember, Christ loved you when you were unlovely. If you honor Him and follow His directions, He will help you succeed. You must put God first. You must show Him as holy. What will this look like in your everyday life and in your everyday talk?

God has charged you with the responsibility of teaching your children about Him all along the road of life. He wants your everyday talk to lead your children to Christ. You are the first and most important teacher your children have about God. He wants you to present Him as a holy God to your children. There is no better opportunity to do this than when your children sin against you. How is that?

Let's look at Moses' relationship with Israel as a parent-child model for this particular issue. His relationship with the Israelites bears some similarities to your relationship with your children. Consider this:

- Moses was charged with leading Israel out of slavery in Egypt to freedom in Canaan. God handed Moses an infant nation that was virtually born as it passed through the waters of the Red Sea. Israel could not feed herself, she could not defend herself, she did not know how to do what was right. The job of raising Israel to maturity fell to Moses.

- Israel whined and pouted when things were difficult.

- Israel did not like the food that God provided for her.

- Israel constantly chose to do what she wanted rather than what Moses taught her to do. No matter how faithful Moses was in caring for her, Israel always seemed to doubt him.

Parent, does this sound familiar? Can you identify with what Moses faced every day?

You can learn much from how Moses handled the sins of Israel against him. Moses can help teach you how to be a holy parent.

In Numbers 14, God told Israel to enter the land of Canaan

and occupy it as her own. Yet after hearing the ominous report from the ten fearful spies about the powerful inhabitants of the land, the Israelites moaned and cried and felt sorry for themselves. They ignored the encouraging counsel of the other two spies, Joshua and Caleb. Notice how despairing the Israelites are:

That night all the people of the community raised their voices and wept aloud. All the Israelites grumbled against Moses and Aaron, and the whole assembly said to them,

If only we had died in Egypt! Or in this desert! Why is
the Lord bringing us to this land only to let us fall by the
sword? Our wives and children will be taken as plunder.
Wouldn't it be better for us to go back to Egypt?" And
they said to each other, "We should choose a leader and go
back to Egypt. (Numbers 14:1–4)

Moses attempted to encourage Israel by reminding them of God's faithfulness to them since they left Egypt. The people's response was, "Stone Moses and Aaron!"

Consider this from the viewpoint of Moses and Aaron. Moses had faithfully cared for these people. He had been used by God to rescue them from the Egyptian army. Did Israel remember that? No! They wanted to stone him! God had performed many miraculous signs through Moses. God had punished previous rebellions against Moses by sending plagues of judgment against them. And then Moses brought the people to the Promised Land. After all that, the people were afraid and wanted Moses and Aaron stoned to death!

Suppose you were Moses? The Israelites wanted you dead. What would you think? Would you feel justified in expressing some well-deserved self pity? Would it be okay for you to be angry at the Israelites and their ungrateful, complaining spirit?

Even God appeared to have had it with the people:

> But the whole assembly talked about stoning them. Then
> the glory of the LORD appeared at the Tent of Meeting
> to all the Israelites. The LORD said to Moses, "How long
> will these people treat me with contempt? How long will
> they refuse to believe in me, in spite of all the miracu-
> lous signs I have performed among them? I will strike
> them down with a plague and destroy them, but I will
> make you into a nation greater and stronger than they.
> (Numbers 14:10–12)

Obviously, Moses would have been justified in giving up
in anger and frustration at such people. Even God had given
up on them. Or would he? Notice what Moses says to God in
response:

> Moses said to the LORD, "Then the Egyptians will hear
> about it! By your power you brought these people up
> from among them. And they will tell the inhabitants of
> this land about it. They have already heard that you, O
> LORD, are with these people and that you, O LORD,
> have been seen face to face, that your cloud stays over
> them, and that you go before them in a pillar of cloud by
> day and a pillar of fire by night. If you put these people
> to death all at one time, the nations who have heard this
> report about you will say, 'The LORD was not able to
> bring these people into the land he promised them on
> oath; so he slaughtered them in the desert.'
>
> Now may the Lord's strength be displayed, just as you
> have declared: 'The LORD is slow to anger, abounding in

love and forgiving sin and rebellion. Yet he does not leave the guilty unpunished; he punishes the children for the sin of the fathers to the third and fourth generation.' In accordance with your great love, forgive the sin of these people, just as you have pardoned them from the time they left Egypt until now.'
(Numbers 14:13–19)

What was Moses' concern? He was concerned about the honor and reputation of his God. He appealed to God to forgive these people. WHY? Was it because the Israelites had been mostly good? Was it because Israel would feel bad if God rebuked them, and they would think that God didn't like them anymore? No, Moses was concerned about the honor of God's Name. On this basis he pled for Israel. God heard Moses and honored his request, even though God did carry out judgment on those who had been so doubting. But God preserved the people as Moses asked.

Would you have responded the same way in this situation? Or would you have been tempted to tell God, "Why sure, Lord, I would be honored to start a new nation for you." But if you had done so, you would have been ordinary. What Moses did was not ordinary, it was holy. Moses showed the people that God was holy. He did not call for their punishment. He cried out to God, urging God to forgive them for the sake of His honor. Moses was not reacting to the fact that he had been slandered and threatened with death. He was more concerned about the honor of his friend, the Lord God of Hosts. Moses, acting as God's representative, showed that God was a holy God and worthy of praise. God was not ordinary like man. God was special—more patient, more merciful, more loving than ordinary men would ever be. God was holy.

This point is underscored later on when the people once again started to complain because they had no water. Even after all the times that God had cared for them and met their needs, they doubted God and wanted to go back to Egypt. They said, "If only we had died when God struck down our brothers. Why did you bring us out here to die of thirst?"

Moses and Aaron again went before God to ask for direction. Only this time the frustration of the people's sin got the best of Moses. God told Moses to speak to the rock and the water would come out. Instead, Moses responded in a way that an ordinary leader would have done. He picked up his rod and, in anger and frustration, he struck the rock. He called the people rebels, which was true—they were. But in his anger he forgot about God's honor and focused only on himself and his frustrations. He lashed out at the people and, in the process, presented God as ordinary, like the people.

> So Moses took the staff from the LORD's presence, just as he commanded him. He and Aaron gathered the assembly together in front of the rock and Moses said to them, "Listen, you rebels, must we bring you water out of this rock?" Then Moses raised his arm and struck the rock twice with his staff. Water gushed out, and the community and their livestock drank.

> But the LORD said to Moses and Aaron, "Because you did not trust in me enough to honor me as holy in the sight of the Israelites, you will not bring this community into the land I give them." (Numbers 20:9–12)

By acting in an ordinary, understandable way, Moses represented God as being like him and not holy. Any human can react in frustration and anger at sinful behavior. Moses lost sight of the honor of God and was therefore quite ordinary in his actions. But God is not ordinary. He is holy.

Parents, when your children sin and they are not respectful to you, how do you want to respond? If you make the matter primarily a personal offense against yourself and respond in anger and frustration, you will do what any ordinary parent might do. You might get angry at them. You might just let your children know how painful this is for you. You might yell. You might walk around in silent pain. You might tell your kids they have gone too far this time. All these responses would be ordinary and totally understandable. In this way you would associate God with the ordinary actions of ordinary people.

"But," you might protest, "what else can you expect me to do after such a painful experience? It's hard, and I'm only human!"

Of course it is hard. Your tears of hurt are real. But God is the God of all comfort. Christ can help just when you need him. Therefore, as parents, you must prepare for what you don't expect. No parent looks forward to his child being disrespectful and unkind. But you must assume it will happen and plan for it. If you are not prepared, you will not focus on how God wants you to respond to your children. You will focus more on your own hurt than on showing God as holy and loving to your children. You hurt. You are angry. You have been sinned against. You have not been appreciated or respected. This is all your children and others will see—how much you have been hurt. It will be all about you.

However, God wants you to respond the way Moses did the first time, in Numbers 14. God wants you to have a holy response. If your focus is on yourself, you will have an ordinary response, as Moses did the second time, in Numbers 20. He wants your everyday talk to focus on God's honor and God's holiness. Why? There are at least two reasons.

First, because God must be honored in love in all that we do. Second, because your children need to be taught how extraordinary, how holy and wonderful God is.

In Numbers 20, Moses' anger got in the way of the real problem. The people were not trusting God to provide water for them. They got mad at Moses. Moses responded as if the problem were only between himself and the people. Yes, the people were ungrateful, forgetful and disrespectful to Moses. But Moses forgot he was not the main figure. The central figure was God. When Moses got angry, yelled at the camp and struck the rock, he made himself the center of the problem. But God was really at the center. The people were not trusting God. Moses lost sight of the reality that he was there to serve God. When Moses focused on himself, he became ordinary, just like the world around him.

Parents, when you give in to anger, resentment or self-pity at your children's bad behavior, you make yourself the center of the problem. You are loving yourself first and most. You must love your kids enough to show them the danger of their behavior. They need to see that their first problem is with God, and only secondarily with you, as we saw in the previous chapter. You must be more concerned for them than for yourself, and you must be concerned most of all for God. By modeling patience, love, self-control—and all the fruit of the Spirit—you teach your children how extraordinary God is.

This was the issue with Moses and Israel, too. God, not Moses, was the one in authority. Moses' authority was to act as God's agent. Israel was accountable to God, not Moses. When Moses lashed out at the people and struck the rock, he made himself the center. This indicated that the representative of God (Moses) and, therefore, God Himself was quite ordinary:

"You don't do what I want so I get mad." (This is the ordinary response.)

However, in Numbers 14 Moses pled for the people in a similar situation of rebellion and dishonor. That time Moses trusted God and acted to preserve the people. That was not an ordinary response. On the first occasion Moses illustrated that God was not like man but, rather, holy. In Numbers 20, however, God characterized Moses' outburst as a lack of trust.

Trust must be practiced; it is not automatic. To show God as holy requires trust. Often it is not easy. That is why you must prepare for your children's bad behavior. You must respond to sin in a way that honors God first, even when all your emotional responses are telling you to lash out or to give up. Trusting God when you are sinned against is an act of holiness. In your every-day life there will come times when your children's sin takes you by surprise. Prepare for that day so that your talk will show your God to be a holy God. Make your everyday talk holy, not ordinary.

Application Questions

1. Make a list of your own typical "ordinary responses" to your child's sin that fall short of God's standard. (You could refer to I Corinthians 13 for one reminder of God's standard).

2. When righteous anger toward your child's sin is appropriate, how can you honor God and benefit your child in the way you express your anger? Give specific examples.

3. List some examples in which God has not treated you in an "ordinary" way for your sins.

Six

Big Sins, Little Sins

Everyday talk, everyday listening, everyday directions. these activities define your parenting style. They reveal whether your parenting is ordinary or holy. What is important to you will dominate your thinking. The way that you talk and listen and give directions shows what is important to you.

Are the things that are important to you also important to God? This is an easy way to summarize what it means to be holy as opposed to being ordinary. If your mind is focused on what the world says is important, then you are ordinary. However, if you are focused on what God says is important, then you have taken a vital step toward holiness. When you are continually trying to line up your priorities with God's priorities, your everyday talk will be transformed into everyday talk that pleases God.

We have already discussed how to give directions and how to respond when your children sin against you. Perhaps by now you are thinking, "Okay, I know to speak pleasantly; I know I should always respond in love rather than impatience and anger. BUT, God did punish the Israelites eventually. They did have to suffer for their rebellion and disobedience. When do I finally get around to consequences and discipline?"

Good question! To answer it, let's back up a little. A holy response to your child's sin is not a substitute for discipline; rather, it is simply the way you talk when you discipline. It enhances discipline. It enables you to exercise discipline most effectively.

An ordinary, exasperated response clouds the discipline issue because it focuses at least some, if not all, the attention on the parent's reaction. The child is busy avoiding his parent's wrath, either literally or figuratively. In contrast, a holy, self-controlled response goes right to the heart of the problem, the child's sin against God, and forces him to deal with that issue.

You cannot discipline properly until you see yourself as God's agent to your kids;

Both you and they are accountable first of all to God. Let me say it again:

1. Your children are accountable to God for their obedience to you, and

2. you are accountable to God for raising your children to fear Him.

Therefore, your focus in discipline is to hold your children accountable to God (cf. chart on page 41).

Those two facts should control your parenting priorities. "Children, obey your parents in the Lord, for this is right." This is basic training. Most Christian parents will not argue with this. However, more often than not, parents do not enforce this command consistently, either from ignorance or to serve their own convenience. To the extent they are inconsistent, they do not help their child grow in obedience and love to God.

"**When do I discipline?** What issues are important enough to discipline for, and what issues do I overlook?" Many parents struggle with this question; because they have no consistent basis for discipline, the question comes up again and again.

Let me illustrate what I mean. In this example, four-year-old Andrew is running through the house. Michelle is on the phone as he flies by the kitchen table. He stumbles, piling into the table and knocking off a plastic cup full of water. Michelle picks him up, makes sure that he is okay and tells him not to worry, it was only water that spilled. He smiles, Michelle smiles, gives him a pat on the head and resumes her phone conversation. Even though Michelle told him not to run through the kitchen a million times before, she doesn't mention that to him this time; after all, it was only a cup of water, and she's in the middle of a conversation.

The next day Michelle is again at her kitchen table talking on the phone. This time, however, she is cleaning her fine crystal stemware. Andrew again races through, stumbles, piles into the table and knocks a piece of her fine crystal to the floor, where it shatters. Andrew looks up with a small smile, expecting the same result as yesterday. Instead, Michelle hangs up the phone and angrily tells Andrew that he has really done it this time.

"How many times have I told you not to run in the house? Now look what you've done! Do you know how expensive that was?" Andrew starts crying. He is confused. Yesterday, what seemed to be the same thing was treated as if it didn't matter. Today, he is a monster. Yesterday, a little sin was overlooked. Today, a big sin is punished.. Big sins, little sins.

What was the difference between the two events? The first time the only apparent damage was spilled water, certainly nothing to engage in discipline over. The second time the damage was a shattered piece of treasured crystal. But think about this with me. What was the real sin? Was it not Andrew running when he was told not to? Yet Michelle is concerned enough to discipline only when a major loss of crystal occurs. You see, the wrong comparison here is the shattered crystal and the spilled water. Both are the results of Andrew's disobedience and Michelle's failure to require obedience. Ordinary things are too important to Michelle. Whatever is important to God is holy. If you distinguish this way between little sins and big sins, your thinking is not holy, but ordinary.

God does not have a category of big sins (those which a parent gets really upset about), and little sins (those which the parent will usually ignore).

God wants to be loved and obeyed at all times, not just when the consequences seem great to us. You must discipline your children every time they are disobedient. As God's agent, you do not have the right to excuse or ignore disobedience. God requires you to bring up your children in the fear of the Lord. You may not make obedience a trivial or occasional issue. When a child deliberately disobeys, you have no choice but to exercise discipline out of love for God and love for your child.[1]

You can easily see how this "big sins, little sins" mentality profoundly influences your everyday talk. Since the first incident was only about spilled water, nothing really registered on the parent's radar screen. The phone call was important. But in reality, what was of greater importance was that Andrew was disobeying his mother and, therefore, God (remember Ephesians 6:1) by running where he was told not to. If Michelle had been concerned about the seriousness of disobedience, Andrew would have been disciplined the first time. Not for spilling the water, but for running when he was not supposed to. Perhaps the second incident with the shattered crystal would never have happened if Andrew had been properly challenged the day before.

It is dangerous to judge the seriousness of sin by the consequences.

Andrew was being equally disobedient in both circumstances. Yet the first time, when the consequences were minimal, there was no rebuke, only a smile and, "Hey, no problem." Perhaps Mom even gave herself a pat on the back for being so patient and kind and not getting upset. In the second circumstance, the consequences were substantial and so was Andrew's discipline. Yet Andrew's sin was no worse the second time than the first. He ran when he was not supposed to.

Big sins or little sins? If Michelle had been seriously concerned about Andrew's obedience she would have seen the running as a big deal. The conversation that Andrew's mom had with him immediately after each incident is an example of the profound importance of everyday talk. In both situations she did not really think much about what she said. She reacted with speech that was consistent with what was important to her. The first time, the phone call was most important and spilled water was not important. Therefore, her everyday talk reflected those priorities. *Let's make sure Andrew is all right so I can get back to the phone call.* If training Andrew to love God had been the most important thing (Deuteronomy 6:7), then she would have seen the running as a big deal and gotten off the phone to confront and discipline him about his disobedience. Her immediate reaction revealed what was important to her. Such incidents demonstrate whether the "big sins, little sins" mindset is at work.

In the second incident Michelle was angry because of the cost of the crystal. Her immediate words to Andrew reflect that value.

But as valuable as crystal is, it pales in comparison to the value of loving God with all your heart. Andrew was dishonoring God by disobeying his parents' direction. Andrew's mom was dishonoring God because she did not help Andrew see the importance of obedience. Her everyday talk exposed her values. Andrew will likely remember this event as the time he got in really big trouble for breaking the crystal. However, of greater importance is the fact that Andrew was not loving God by obeying Michelle. The real sin in this scenario was lost amidst the pieces of shattered crystal.

The consequences of sin are not always quickly known. Some consequences are immediately predictable, like jumping out of an airplane without a parachute. But most of the time the consequences are harder to discern. If Andrew decides to disobey and run he can't really know if he will spill water or break crystal or be undetected. The danger is to decide based upon which consequence is most likely. If Andrew thinks he might break some crystal and get in big trouble and decides not to run for that reason, he has not made a decision to love God but, rather, to protect himself. This is not the everyday obedience that God desires, it is self-interest.

It doesn't take too much imagination to apply this example to other situations. If you think you might get a speeding ticket, then you probably won't speed. If you think that by speeding you can get to work on time, then you might speed. Making a decision on these two factors alone is not serving God; it is serving yourself. This is an example of the "big sins, little sins" mentality.

Let's try another example. Kevin, a young teenage boy has an opportunity to be alone with Tiffany, a girl from school with a reputation of being sexually active. If he thinks that he might get caught alone with her and his parents will find out, or that he might get a sexually-transmitted disease from this girl, he might decide not to be alone with her. However, suppose she successfully entices him into thinking that no one will find out (see Proverbs 7) and that a little fun never hurt anyone. He might be persuaded to be alone with her. This is an example of the "big sins, little sins" way of thinking. In both of these examples the consequences are influencing the actions. What is the best way to love God is not even a consideration.

Parent, when you discipline for "big sins" and overlook "little sins" you are setting a bad example for your children.

Your are teaching them, by your own example, to obey only when it seems necessary to them. You are teaching them it is okay to disobey if they don't get caught. You are showing them that pleasing God is not really very important—certainly not worth much inconvenience or self-denial.

One day, four-year-old Andrew will become fourteen-year-old Andrew. What will keep him from falling into the trap of the sexual temptation? If he is only choosing his actions based upon how serious he thinks the consequences will be, he is a sitting duck. When temptation is teasing and luring him, he will gamble his life that the consequences will be only spilled water, not broken crystal. But if he is thinking of what will please and honor God, then he will receive the protection this holy sort of thinking provides.

Proverbs 6:20-24 teaches you this way of thinking:

> My son, keep your father's commands and do not forsake
> your mother's teaching. Bind them upon your heart
> forever; fasten them around your neck.

When you walk, they will guide you; when you sleep,
they will watch over you; when you awake, they will
speak to you.

For these commands are a lamp, this teaching is a light,
and the corrections of discipline are the way to life,

keeping you from the immoral woman, from the smooth
tongue of the wayward wife. (Proverbs 6:20-24)

"Big sins, little sins" thinking will not offer the protection
these verses offer.

Your everyday talk must reflect a deep concern for loving
and serving God through everyday obedience. If you show your
children that your decisions are based upon the seriousness of
consequences, you will lead them into the "big sins, little sins"
way of thinking. If Andrew learns that he is really loving and
pleasing God by obeying you by not running in the house, then
he will be protected by his love for God and His Word. This
mindset is the result of everyday talk—day after day, year after
year—that presents pleasing God as the highest goal and desire.

Your instructions to your children about how to live in your
home day by day must reflect your deep concern to honor God. In
Deuteronomy 6 God says that the things of God are to dominate
your thinking. You are to impress His commands on your
children by talking to them every day about these commands.
That should get your attention as a parent.

When you give directions it should not be for selfish reasons.

For example, "I want the house to be quiet so I will teach
the children not to run inside." Rather, you should be persuaded

that a particular command will help your children learn to honor God. Your reasoning might be like something like this:

"A quiet house will help all of us be more orderly and show consideration for others. Also, running in tight quarters might be dangerous. I know these things are pleasing to God, so we will make a rule that we will not run in the house. If this direction is disobeyed, it is a serious matter, because God is not being honored."

In the example of Andrew and Michelle, running was not treated as a big deal. It was a good rule for the house, yet the command was not enforced until a bad consequence happened. You should make your rules thoughtfully and carefully, based on biblical principles of behavior, and then enforce them consistently. It is better to make a few basic rules that you enforce rather than have too many rules to keep up with.

How do I discipline?

This is often the next question after, "When do I discipline?" This book, however, is about talk—everyday talk. A number of important aspects of childrearing are outside the scope of this topic. While I am tempted to discuss the "how to" of discipline, I will not do so here. Instead, I refer you to several books that address this particular issue in a biblical and practical way: *Christian Living in the Home* by Jay Adams (P&R Publishing Company), *Teach Them Diligently* by Lou Priolo (Timeless Texts), *Withhold Not Correction* by Bruce Ray (P&R Publishing), and *Shepherding a Child's Heart* by Tedd Tripp (Shepherd Press).

Let's look at one more biblical passage that contains a shocking example of a defective view of sin. Let's look at Matthew 19:16-22

And someone came to Him and said, "Teacher, what good thing shall I do that I may obtain eternal life?"

And He said to him, "Why are you asking Me about what is good? There is only One who is good; but if you wish to enter into life, keep the commandments."

Then he said to Him, "Which ones?" And Jesus said, **"you shall not commit murder; you shall not commit adultery; you shall not steal; you shall not bear false witness; honor your father and mother; and you shall love your neighbor as yourself."**

The young man said to Him, "All these things I have kept; what am I still lacking?"

Jesus said to him, "If you wish to be complete, go and sell your possessions and give to the poor, and you will have treasure in heaven; and come, follow Me."

But when the young man heard this statement, he went away grieving; for he was one who owned much property. NASB

What kind of a young man was this? According to his own testimony, he was a rather good young man. He began the conversation with Christ by asking what he could do to obtain eternal life. It appears from the text that his interest in eternal life was focused on consequences rather than loving God. The young man had reasoned that heaven is far more desirable than hell, so he wanted to know how to obtain heaven. Jesus addressed the heart of his concerns. Jesus said, "If you want to enter into life, keep the commandments."

The young man most probably answered with eagerness as he asked, "Which ones?" He knew that he had kept the outward form of all of them. He was blind to the goal of the commandments, which is loving God with all of one's heart. In any event, he was most likely thrilled with Jesus' answer because he thought he had kept them all. He had been a child and a young man who had been outwardly obedient. He answered with a telling confidence. He had kept them all.

Now, if he had attempted to keep them from the heart, as Jesus defined them, he would have realized his failure to obey the Law. He, and probably his parents as well, had made the Law ordinary. They had bought into an interpretation of the Law that made it achievable. This young man had figured out what big sins should be avoided. He thought himself to be quite holy; however, in God's eyes he was quite ordinary. In his misplaced confidence he offered a challenging appeal to Christ. "What else do I lack?"

Christ's response ended his self-confidence and exposed his focus on consequences rather than on true obedience. Christ exposed his lack of love for God and showed his self-love. Jesus said that what he had to do was to sell all that he had and give it to the poor and come and follow Him. Such a simple thing to do. Sell everything, give it to those in need and come and be with Jesus. Yet the consequences of this request were too much for the young man. He was rich. He would have to give up the comforts and prestige that he loved. The consequences were too much to bear. He left Jesus, grieving as he went. He had followed the form of faith but not the reality of faith. Loving God was not his reason for keeping the commandments. If loving God had been the true reason for his obedience, then Christ's words would have brought him great joy. He could have gained the daily presence and companionship of Christ! Instead, he grieved because he had too much to lose. The consequences were unacceptable. The Rich Young Ruler was quite ordinary after all.

Parent, how hard would it be for you to have a son like the rich young ruler?

He would be respected by everyone. He would have a reputation as a fine, moral young man. He would be respectful to you, his parents. He would make wise use of his wealth. Everyone would compliment you on your fine, successful son. They would wish their children were as obedient as your son. How hard would it be?

Do you see the danger? Yes, he appeared to be the ideal son. But this young man valued consequences over loving God. When he encountered the living Christ, he turned away towards hell rather than give up what he thought he had. In his mind this young man had committed only little sins, not big sins. He had always made the safe move (cf. Proverbs 1:32). Obedience was good because it made his life easier. He loved the good consequences rather than the good God.

Do not wish for your children to be like the rich young ruler. Don't settle for pleasant consequences and a good report from the world. No one is really that good. Everyone sins and fails. Rather, teach your children by the powerful weapon of your everyday talk to turn from their sin to Christ. Hold out for them the goal of a heart that loves Christ more than the pleasures and good consequences of this life. Ask God to help your everyday talk to reflect love of God more than love of good consequences.

"Big sins, little sins" thinking shows sin as a matter of good or bad consequences. This kind of thinking is self-pleasing and leads to a lack of love for God and His Word. See this for what it is. Examine your everyday talk to see if it reflects love for God or simply a reaction to consequences. Examine your life and language to see if you have bought into the "big sins, little sins" mindset. If you have, turn your eyes, your heart, your life to Jesus. Repent and ask Him to help you change. Ask for the wisdom and strength to love Him with all your heart.

Application Questions

1. What do you think your children would list as "big sins" in your home?

2. What would they list as "little sins?"

3. When are you most likely to enforce the rules of your household? Least likely?

4. What does the previous answer reflect concerning your functional priorities?

Footnotes

[1] Deliberate disobedience and childishness are two different things and should not necessarily receive the same discipline. For the sake of the illustration above, I am assuming that the running was deliberate disobedience.

Thirteen Comes Before Twenty-One

So far we have spent considerable time focusing on the words you say each day to your children. You have seen the power and importance of everyday talk. Now I would like you to consider just how long term the impact of everyday talk is. After all, parenting itself is a long term task. The goal of childrearing is to help your children grow into adults who love and honor God in all of life. It is an awesome task.

You probably have some ideas about your child's future. You could describe the kind of adult you hope he or she will be, at least in general terms. But between now and then will come the teenage years. Thirteen comes before twenty-one, and your children will be teenagers before they are adults. How should you prepare for the teen years?

Parents frequently complain about the difficulty of living with teens—their rebellion, their undesirable friends, bad influences, bad music, moodiness, sullenness, etc. Too often, that description is accurate.

In the first chapter we noted some statistics from *The Index of Leading Cultural Indicators*. Teenagers talk less than thirty-five minutes a week with their fathers. In contrast, these same teenagers watch twenty-one hours of television each week. Picture these statistics as a sports box score:

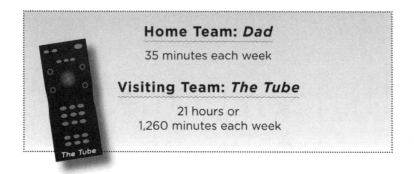

Home Team: *Dad*

35 minutes each week

Visiting Team: *The Tube*

21 hours or
1,260 minutes each week

It doesn't take much to figure out who is winning and who is losing this battle for influence. For every one minute a teenager talks with Dad, he spends thirty-six minutes with the TV. The visitors are cleaning up.

There is no question that the above number reveals a breakdown between parents and their children. Teenagers greatly need good counsel. Yet in family after family, teenagers seldom seek the counsel of parents. Tensions often run high. Mistrust is common. Conversations are short, evasive and aggravating. It is easy to understand why the home team loses so often.

Most of you know families with good relationships between parents and teenagers. You may even point them out as uncommon. Sadly, this underscores the concern; good relationships are unusual. You do not need any detailed studies to tell you that the teenage years are difficult ones for teenagers and their parents. The question is, "Does it have to be this way?"

No, it doesn't.

If you have young children you can prepare now for the years ahead by your everyday talk. Everyday talk is one important tool that parents have to keep the lines of communication open between themselves and their teenagers-to-be. If you already have teenagers and things are sometimes (or often) rocky, examine your everyday talk to see whether you are using this tool to help or to hinder your relationship with your growing kids.

For your everyday talk to be the successful tool that God wants it to be, you must be responsive to the differences that seem to emerge each day as your children grow into adulthood. Each new set of daily experiences adds another dimension to your child. My oldest son is twenty-four. Yet I can still see him, in my mind, when we brought him home from the hospital as a newborn. Many changes have taken place in his life since then. I can no longer treat him as an infant, a toddler, a young child, or now, as a teenager. All parents have to learn to adapt to these changes in order for everyday talk to help effectively as children grow to be mature young people who love God. While this is simple enough to understand in theory, the point is often lost in everyday life. Simply put, your everyday talk must change in style and in content as your children grow older. For example, "It is time to go to bed right now," may work just fine for your three-year-old. However, your twelve-year-old may be an entirely different story.

You might answer, "Why should there be a difference? A command is a command, and my child should obey regardless of what age he is, whether he is three or twelve."

It is true that a child should obey, but remember that you also have the responsibility to present commands as precious gifts from God (cf. Proverbs 1:8–9). You must work to make your directions—your everyday talk—desirable, attractive and wise. In short, you must consider your listener with great care when giving directions. Your primary concern must be to help the hearer, your child. Your primary consideration is not to give what you think are clear commands. You may be clear, but you also may be exasperating your child. Clarity is only one consideration. God wants you to understand the impact that your words have on others, including your children. This principle is taught in Ephesians 4:29 and has significant implications for parental instruction. I have listed three translations to help you grasp the full impact of this pivotal passage.

> Let no unwholesome word proceed from your mouth, but only such a word as is good for edification according to the need of the moment, so that it will give grace to those who hear. NASB

> Do not let any unwholesome talk come out of your mouths, but only what is helpful for building others up according to their needs, that it may benefit those who listen. NIV

> Don't let a single rotten word come from your mouth, but rather, whatever is good for constructively meeting problems that arise, so that your words may help those who hear. CCNT[1]

Let's look at this verse carefully. Both the New International Version and the New American Standard use the word *unwholesome* to translate the word found in the original Greek, *sapros*. The word certainly does mean *unwholesome,* but in the original it is a stronger expression than it is in our everyday speech. *The Linguistic Key to the Greek New Testament*[2] says that *sapros,* the word translated *unwholesome,* means "rank, foul, putrid, rotten, worthless, disgusting." You can see that the Greek word carries more force than *unwholesome* in everyday speech. The CCNT translation is closer to the mark by using the word *rotten* for *sapros.*

So what kind of language is it that Paul considers "rotten, foul, rank, disgusting?" Well, this would certainly include cursing or swearing. But again, much more is meant by Paul. Look closely; Paul is making a contrast. He is saying, "Don't speak rotten words, but rather with words that build up and benefit the hearer." So, if your language does not benefit your listener it may be considered rotten language. Paul, as is typical of him, doesn't leave any middle ground here. He directs us to use only words that build up. He says, "Let no rotten words be used, but only words that build up according to the need of the moment." From the context of this verse, then, it is fair to say that what Paul considers to be a rotten word is *any* word that does not benefit the hearer so as to build him up. This covers much, much more than just four-letter words. It includes all those words that tear down.

Paul's direction to you, parent, means that you must understand how your words will impact your child. Are you aware of speech patterns that you have that will exasperate your child? Will your direction be received as demeaning from your child's perspective? If it will, then your language can be classified as unwholesome and rotten at that point because it does not benefit your listener. Paul says in 2 Corinthians 13:10 that the purpose of authority is to build up and not tear down. You must carefully consider whether your everyday talk to your kids is building them up. This means that God wants you to be aware of how your children are responding to your words. It is easy to focus on what you want your children to do or not do. But you must also be concerned with how your direction impacts your children.

For example, ten-year-old Caitlin has had a bad day. Some friends were unkind to her at church. She has discovered that she is no longer considered to be "in" with some of the popular girls. She is sad and despondent around the house. Her dad doesn't know why she is "down," but reasons that she needs to snap out of it. So he says something like, "Caitlin, it is not good for you to be so down. You attitude is discouraging everyone else in the house. God wants you to be happy and pleasant to others. So, I want you to exercise some self-control and stop being so sad right now. Okay? It is time for you to snap out of this."

Now, even though everything he said was true, these words were not helpful, but rotten. Caitlin should not be down and gloomy. She does need to remember that she has much to be thankful to God for. Yet these words, spoken in this context, constitute rotten words. These words were spoken without any attempt to listen first, to understand what would benefit Caitlin in her struggle at the moment. There was no attempt to find out why she was sad. For a child Caitlin's age, finding out suddenly that she is being excluded from the group of girls she thought were friends is devastating. Saying things that are true but not appropriate to the situation will lead to a breakdown in communication and in relationship. Once Dad is able to understand what Caitlin is struggling with, he can begin to bring the right scriptural principles to bear.

Parents, this is where frustration often takes root in a parent's relationship with his growing children. He says things that he knows are true and should be helpful. He becomes upset when he sees that his words are met with silence, anger or indifference. His child, on the other hand, is also frustrated. She is hurting from apparently being tossed aside by her friends. This is all that she can think about. All Dad can do is spout rules. Dad doesn't know and Dad doesn't care. This kind of breakdown can lead to some rough times ahead. At least part of the solution is speaking words that helpfully meet the problem of the moment.

So Ephesians 4:29 has much to say about how to talk with your children. You must use words that consider the needs of your child so that he is helped by them.

Now, having laid this groundwork, let's return to the theme for this chapter. Age thirteen is an important milestone in the life of your child. At this age your child becomes a teenager. He or she is beginning to emerge into adulthood. These years are difficult; the process of maturing from child to adult is challenging. Think of all that has to happen in a few short years. The parent-child relationship must change from total dependence, obedience and submission to relative independence; respect and honor instead of immediate obedience; and unmediated accountability to God and church, apart from the parents.

This is a drastic change. Sometime it seems that within mere moments your child has left home and been replaced with this teenager person. This person is the same one that was born some thirteen years earlier.[2] But he is also quite different. The "switch" to teenager is often traumatic for all concerned. The parents really weren't expecting him and often neither was the teenager. So everyone may be surprised. The new teenager is feeling, thinking, wondering, exploring about things that are new to him as well. New things are happening to his body. Hair is growing in new places. A boy's voice changes. The body takes on a different shape. It also changes on the inside and is now ready to produce children. Body chemistry is different. Life is different. Imagine the following scenario.

Suppose I told you that you were going to have a house guest in your home thirteen years from now. This house guest would most likely be quite different from the people now in your home. You would not have the option to decide whether or not this new guest would come. You would be required to provide all of his support and be responsible for his actions as soon as he comes into your home. He might be argumentative and selfish. Furthermore, this new guest would be residing in your home for at least six years. Remember, you don't have a choice as to whether this new guest comes or not.

What would you do?

Well, you might ask me for some background data so that you can know what to expect when he arrives. That's a good idea, but I would have to respond and say, "Honestly, I don't know what he will be like. You see, the next thirteen years will be critical in determining that. So I really won't know until he gets here. But let me warn you, if things don't go well in this person's life for the next thirteen years, things could be pretty miserable for the next six years he is with you."

So you think again for a few minutes and ask me, "Well if the next thirteen years are so critical to what our life will be like for the next six years after he comes, would it be possible for him to come live with us now? That way we could start working with him now so that things might not be so terrible when he does come."

Of course you get the point. The new house guest is obviously the teenager that your child will grow up to become. My point is that we seldom connect our immediate actions with the distant future. With a few exceptions, our culture focuses on the immediate, the now.

Any college or professional sports coach who presented a ten-year plan for putting his team on top would lose his job immediately. Why? Because the fans, the owners and the media all want to win now! Imagine a politician who ran for office on this platform: "Things will be difficult for awhile. It will take months and, in some cases, years for our programs to produce the change we need. I have no immediate solution to your problems. All I can offer you is that I will encourage you to work hard for a long time." Or how about a TV ad that proclaimed: "Don't live for the moment. Dress for the future. Our new durable fabric means that our shirts will last at least ten years. Imagine that! You won't have to replace our great shirt for ten years! Don't worry about fashion trends anymore. Ten years from now you can still be wearing the same shirt!"

Such thoughts are foreign to life in 21st century America. This culture of the immediate has influenced our family structure as well. Life has become a blur of Little League practices and games, piano lessons, birthday parties, tests in school, homework due in the morning, doctor's and dentist's appointments, holidays just around the corner, vacations, cutting grass, shoveling snow, getting the car out of the shop, going to school, getting to work, etc. In all of this it is easy to forget about the teenager who will be coming to live in your home.

Your everyday talk in the middle of the rush of life, perhaps more than any other single factor, will determine what life with your teenager will be like. God wants your everyday talk to center on more than just what it takes to meet the next event deadline.

For ten-year-old Caitlin, hearing you dispense true statements that seem to be disconnected from her life will make for a rocky arrival for the teenage Caitlin. She will be convinced that you don't understand her or really know her. That is why we studied what the Bible says about having active ears, ears that seek out knowledge about your children. To be a parent who is holy and not ordinary means truly understanding what rotten words are. Paul warns parents not to exasperate their children. Speaking words that are true but not relevant or helpful is one sure way to exasperate your children.

As your child matures, your everyday talk will have more to do with your influence and wise counsel than with commands and obedience. Your everyday listening will require patience and humility as you give your kids room to think through issues and formulate their own attitudes and decisions. This can be both difficult and rewarding.

The groundwork for the teen years is laid during the first twelve years. This may seem quite obvious, but the parents of toddlers and young children rarely take time to think much about what's coming in five or ten years. They are too busy trying to keep up with the here and now. The skills we have discussed in the first six chapters—listening, talking, presenting the gospel, understanding sin and obedience—these skills will equip you to make that transition through the teen years. I said these years are difficult, but let me say emphatically, difficult doesn't equal bad. These years can be a wonderful time of growing friendships with your young adult children.

When you grow weary of the daily demands of everyday talk, *don't give up!* Remember that what you say and do now, day by day, has a lifelong impact on your children. By God's grace, you and they will reap the benefit in the years ahead.

Listen again to your friend, the apostle Paul, "Don't let a single rotten word come from your mouth, but rather, whatever is good for constructively meeting problems that arise, so that your words may help those who hear" (CCNT).

This one direction from the Holy Spirit is the driving force behind the whole biblical concept of everyday talk. You want your words to build up your children. You want to say helpful things when problems unexpectedly arise, as they almost always seem to do. To avoid rotten words, God wants you to listen actively and speak with the power of pleasant words; in short, don't be ordinary, be holy.

Remember, thirteen comes before twenty-one. Will you be ready?

Application Questions

1. What inappropriate behaviors do you expect your young children to "grow out of" by their teens? Are these developmental issues (childishness) or sin/obedience issues?

2. List conversations (if applicable) during which your teenager said that you "didn't understand." What can you do to change that assessment—without arguing about it?

3. What lifestyle decisions and responsibilities will you allow your teenager to handle for himself—even if his choices differ from yours—and when?

Footnotes

[1] Jay E. Adams, trans. *The Christian Counselors New Testament,* (Stanley, NC: Timeless Texts, 1977).

[2] *The Linguistic Key to the Greek New Testament,* Rienecker / Rogers page 534.

[3] The age thirteen is somewhat symbolic. This new and different person may arrive anywhere from the age of twelve to fifteen, depending upon the child.

Eight

Your Home is God's Greenhouse

A greenhouse is defined as a structure in which the environment can be controlled for the cultivation or protection of plants.[1] A greenhouse is good for plants. It provides a safe environment for growing seedlings into strong, healthy, mature plants. Then, when the plants are developed enough, the gardener prepares them gradually for the transition to the outside. In the end, they can thrive and grow in the natural environment.

A greenhouse is also good for children. No, I don't mean that you should raise your children in a humid glass house and water them with a sprinkler system each day! Nor do I mean that you should shelter them from any exposure to sin or sinners (as if you could!). However, the purpose of a greenhouse is similar to the purpose of your home. As a greenhouse is used for the cultivation of plants, your home is used to cultivate faith in Christ for your children. Your home should provide spiritual protection from the harsh storms of daily life.

Jesus underscores this point in Matthew 7:24-27 where he teaches that the storms of life will come for both the wise builder and the foolish builder. The raging winds of this world strike everyone. The question is whether your children will survive the storms. The storms will come even if you have done well in raising your children. No system or methodology of parenting will prevent the storms. God's purpose for your greenhouse, your home, is to prepare, protect and cultivate. Your home should protect them from the harsh, hostile realities of the world until they are sufficiently prepared to withstand the attacks they will face. Eventually, when they have been taught and trained in the home and church, they will be equipped to survive and grow in the rich soil of God's word.

That is why Ephesians 4:29 is such an important tool for parents. You want your words to protect and benefit your children so they will be ready to face a hostile world with God's power. The biblical home has always had the goal to protect, prepare and then send out. In Genesis 2:24 we read, "For this reason a man will leave his father and mother and be united to his wife, and they will become one flesh."

The purpose of the family is 1) to maintain and nourish the one-flesh relationship between husband and wife, and 2) to prepare children to leave the home of their parents and establish their own home. The family does not exist for itself. Genesis 2:24 teaches that the husband-wife relationship does not exist primarily for children. Children are only temporary residents. A husband and wife are to remain together after the children have left. Parents, note this well: God wants your children to leave home. They are to move on. Parents are the ones who stay put.

When children become the primary purpose of family life, the focus of parents shifts to the enjoyment of children. Children become an end in themselves. In the 21st century, children are often wanted simply for the experience of having children. Famous single people, both homosexual and heterosexual, adopt children or bear them outside of marriage because they don't want to miss the parenting experience. To be sure, the Bible teaches that children are a blessing from God. Being a parent should be a profound and wonderful experience. However, this experience must never become the primary goal of having children. They are to be raised for His glory and for His purposes. When people, married or single, Christian or not, have children and raise them for their own purposes, awful consequences occur. Wrong priorities distort the entire concept of family.

This shift in focus from the training of children to the enjoyment of children actually diminishes the pleasure of parenting. Children are selfish, devious and ungrateful by nature. Unless children are instructed and disciplined to follow God, they will follow their own natural ways. They will always frustrate the expectations of parental enjoyment. Parents looking primarily for enjoyment from such creatures are in for a major disappointment. Loving, enjoyable relationships between parents and children are a by-product of good parenting, not the goal. Even at that, the enjoyment of children is a blessing from God that should not be assumed or taken for granted. Many good parents have endured heartbreaking situations with their children.

People like Freud, Dewey, Hall, Spock and Piaget, who despise the very idea of the living God of the Bible, have shaped the world's (and, unfortunately, many Christians') thinking about raising children. These men teach that children are independent beings who must be free to make up their own minds about the world around them. Creativity and discovery must not be stifled. Lies are the expression of a child's mytho-poetic capability.[2] Sexual conduct must not be restricted. Sexual experimentation at almost any age is encouraged. Children must be free to choose what they want to be. Self-expression is the creed of the day, no matter how perverse that expression may be. It does not take long for children raised this way to become anything but enjoyable. Thus child abuse rises, broken homes become the norm and life for many families is an increasing frustration.

In this modern environment, the home functions not as a greenhouse, but as a stage. Children are displayed, not protected. Children are exploited, not trained. Sinful behavior is accepted and defended. Parents live for their children and children live for themselves. Many believe that small children cannot understand such complex concepts as God, sin, responsibility and substitutionary atonement. So instead of teaching children the hope of the gospel as the solution for the difficulties of life, parents invest in their children's accomplishments and performance. If children are not on the honor roll, winning beauty contests or leading the team in scoring at an early age, parents are disappointed. No child can bear this awful weight.

Remember, the home is to be like a greenhouse. Its purpose is to help children grow in God's way. The home is not a stage for displaying children. Over against the modern theme is God's direction for parents to teach children about His ways and how He runs His world. The misunderstanding of this is one reason that the biblical training of children has fallen on hard times. Look carefully at these verses in Proverbs 4:1–6:

Listen, my sons, to a father's instruction;
pay attention and gain understanding.
I give you sound learning,
so do not forsake my teaching.
When I was a boy in my father's house,
still tender, and an only child of my mother,
he taught me and said,
"Lay hold of my words with all your heart;
keep my commands and you will live.
Get wisdom, get understanding;

do not forget my words or swerve from them.
Do not forsake wisdom, and she will protect you;
love her, and she will watch over you.

Sons are told to listen. God says that life is in the balance. Instruction. Wisdom. Learning. Teaching. Obedience. Understanding. These are not the words of the 21st century as it looks at children. But they are God's words. Notice verse six again. "Do not forsake wisdom, and she will protect you; love her, and she will watch over you."

Wisdom will protect children; performance will not.

Proverbs 4 speaks of wisdom that can protect your children when you are not there to direct them and warn them. Love for wisdom will result in protection. This is the theme of the greenhouse: protection and preparation for the life ahead. Proverbs 6:20-24 also echoes and expands upon this theme. Notice carefully the impact of your words as a parent.

My son, keep your father's commands
and do not forsake your mother's teaching.
Bind them upon your heart forever;
fasten them around your neck.

When you walk, they will guide you;
when you sleep, they will watch over you;
when you awake, they will speak to you.
For these commands are a lamp,
this teaching is a light,
and the corrections of discipline
are the way to life,
keeping you from the immoral woman,

from the smooth tongue of the wayward wife.

This passage demonstrates the greenhouse concept. Verse twenty speaks of the everyday talk that both Mom and Dad are to engage in as they instruct children in God's ways. The child is to take this instruction and treat it as the precious gift that it is. The result is that one day, when the child has left the greenhouse and Mom and Dad are not around, these powerful everyday words will protect the young adult from the seductive allure of sexual temptation.

The message of this book is that the most profound teaching your child receives is the everyday talk from your mouth.

Your everyday talk reveals where your treasure is and, therefore, where your heart is. Does love for God dominate your thoughts and your everyday talk? If it does, that talk will watch over and guide your children as Proverbs 6 describes.

Let me apply the greenhouse metaphor to another context. The Jewish leaders in Acts 4 could tell that the apostles had been with Jesus. They had been with him in everyday life. One might even say that the apostles were in a greenhouse with Christ for the three years of His earthly ministry. The apostles had been taught by the everyday talk of Christ. In Acts 4, when Christ was physically absent from the apostles (that is, they had left the greenhouse), His everyday talk had so cultivated their lives that the antagonistic Jewish leaders realized they "had been with Christ." And even the opposition of the Jewish leaders could not turn these men from their mission. As a result of their time with Christ, and by the power of the Holy Spirit, the disciples were sturdy, fruitful Christians.

Remember, the goal for your home is to provide the sort of greenhouse environment that will enable your children to stand in the harsh winds of a world that hates them and their Savior. Obviously, the time comes when children transition out of the home. Just as a gardener hardens his plants gradually to avoid a sudden debilitating shock, wise parents will find ways to expose their children gradually to the outside world.

God wants your home to be a greenhouse that will protect your children while they are young and vulnerable and prepare them thoroughly for the hostile and deceptive world that awaits them.

Application Questions

1. What are some of the dangers and influences of the world from which you should protect your children?

2. According to this chapter, what is the key element that, if present, will protect and strengthen your children in your home?

3. List several examples of 1)specific dangers in the world, and 2) how your home can protect your children from those dangers.

Footnotes

[1] *American Heritage Dictionary of the English Language*, 3rd Edition

[2] G. Stanley Hall as quoted by Daniel Boorstin.

The World:
The Grand Deception

In all of the ease and comfort of modern life it is easy to forget what the world is truly like. It is easy to lose sight of the need to prepare your children for a world which is not their friend. It is easy to love the world. It is so easy that God has given you a clear and dramatic command not to love it.

> Do not love the world nor the things in the world. If anyone loves the world, the love of the Father is not in him. For all that is in the world, the lust of the flesh and the lust of the eyes and the boastful pride of life, is not from the Father, but is from the world. The world is passing away, and also its lusts; but the one who does the will of God lives forever. (1 John 2:15-17)

The apostle John speaks of the world as a hostile place that will turn your children from God. This hostility, however, is often masked by deception. The world does not present itself as a hostile enemy. Rather, the world offers itself as the ultimate source of pleasure, fulfillment and satisfaction. The success of this deception is evident in the lives of many children who have been savaged by the world. Too many children from Christian homes echo the cry of Proverbs 5. Perhaps you, too, have asked these same questions.

> At the end of your life you will groan,
> when your flesh and body are spent.
> You will say, "How I hated discipline!
> How my heart spurned correction!
> I would not obey my teachers
> or listen to my instructors.
> I have come to the brink of utter ruin
> in the midst of the whole assembly." (Proverbs 5:11-14)

Afterward you will groan in anguish when disease consumes your body, and you will say, "How I hated discipline! If only I had not demanded my own way! Oh, why didn't I listen to my teachers? Why didn't I pay attention to those who gave me instruction? I have come to the brink of utter ruin, and now I must face public disgrace" (Proverbs 5:11-14 NLT).

What is the answer to that anguished cry of regret? Why didn't he listen? Why didn't he pay attention?

At least one reason is that he believed the lies, the deceptions of Satan's world. He realized the truth of John's warning too late. As the saying goes, beauty is only skin deep. The world has only the appearance of beauty, not the reality. But the appearance of beauty is alluring and powerful, even though it is false. Satan is hard at work putting an appealing, beautiful veneer over the horrible world that he rules. Never underestimate the danger of false beauty!

Your job as a parent is to use the time while your children are in the protected environment of your home to prepare them for the deceptive, hostile world that they must soon face. The day will come when they must leave behind the protection of your greenhouse. Then they must be strong enough and wise enough to see through Satan's deceit.

The world is not what it appears to be. I have not found a clearer statement of the power of this deception than in the fifth chapter of Jay Adams' book, *Christian Living in the World*. Read carefully the following quotation from that chapter.

> The "world" about which John frequently writes . . . is the kingdom of Satan existing on this planet at any given time, ruled by him and used by him to hinder the progress of the kingdom of God on earth. It is composed of all who have never been redeemed by the blood of Jesus Christ. It is not necessary for them to recognize the fact that they belong to this kingdom, that they serve Satan and his angels and that they oppose God and his kingdom. For the most part, they are blissfully unconscious of the "scattering" in which they engage (cf. Matthew 12:30). That, as a matter of fact, is a large part of what is meant by "the pride of life." The have been lulled into thinking that they are free of all restraints, doing what they want—rather than being ruled by the evil one. His deception, begun in the garden, has continued throughout history. Those who are subject to him believe that they are able to be like God, self-sufficient, autonomous and wise—whereas the opposite is true.
>
> That Satan's subjects are ignorant of the fact that they are members of the kingdom of darkness **is to be expected** [emphasis added]. Ignorance of the truth is characteristic of this kingdom. By the characterization "darkness" [see

Pro. 4:18] Paul intended to signify ignorance as well as sin and death. Satan is the great liar and deceiver (Revelation 12:9). Evidence of this unawareness on the part of the world is clear from the dialog of Christ with the Jews found in John 8. There, the lying protest that they are in bondage to no one (v. 33) is met by Jesus' declaration that they are sin's slave (v.34), that they are children of Satan who carry out his desires (v.44) and that they are estranged from truth (v.45). **One great fact about the world, then, is its near total unawareness of its allegiance to Satan** [emphasis added]. That, of course, is a major achievement of the great Deceiver.

But the believer must never be taken in by Satan's deceptions as are his own followers. Yet, all too often, they are. The world is attractive. As the believer looks at it, desires often arise from what he sees ("the desire of the eyes"). Christians are drawn into its activities by these attractions.[1]

Review with me these points that Dr. Adams makes:

- The world, those who have not been redeemed by Christ, is the kingdom of Satan

- His subjects, for the most part, do not realize that they are under Satan's rule

- His subjects believe they are in charge of their own lives, to do with as they wish

- Because of this deception the world is attractive

Think carefully about these words. You must prepare your children for a world which is deliberately designed to be a milieu of deceit and trickery. This is the world in which your children must be prepared to flourish when they leave your home, your greenhouse.

The world that Satan rules is, in fact, a grand deception. Satan wants to make his world as attractive as it is deceptive. Sexual pleasure, financial independence, exotic vacations, freedom from sickness, powerful stereo systems, professional sports stardom, wide screen TV's, reality computer games, freedom from aging, an exciting career, better golf scores—all hold the promise of fulfillment and contentment. Yet the sales of antidepressant medications continue to rise. Marriages continue to crumble. Young peoples' dreams of sports careers lie shattered in the wake of damaged knees. Frustration with golf games continues to be rampant.

Even when people become aware of the deceit of the world, without Christ they remain captives of the grand deception. Even when they see it for what it is, they cannot break free of it to find truth and freedom. A popular song from 1984 states this reality with chilling accuracy:

I, I live among the creatures of the night
I haven't got the will to try and fight
Against a new tomorrow, so I guess I'll just believe it
That tomorrow never comes

A safe night, I'm living in the forest of my dream
I know the night is not as it would seem
I must believe in something, so I'll make myself believe it
That this night will never go.[2]

Satan has constructed a giant illusion. Even when caught in the awful web of sin, man will naturally choose to follow the deception rather than attempt to break free. In his world, pleasure promises freedom but leads to slavery, and hard work promises fulfillment but often leads only to hard times. This is not what people expect; it is not what the world promises. Yet these promises are part of the grand deception.

To some, the world says that if you work hard you can have what you want in life. Satan delights when someone works hard to accomplish a goal, such as being a successful sports star, only to have it taken away by an injury. He also delights when someone works hard, saves money—and then realizes that it all comes to nothing ultimately. To others, the world says that you don't have to work hard. Take life easy, let the fun come to you. This promise is also a grand deception. Here are some everyday examples:

- Satan's world says that personal peace can be achieved through the death of an unborn child.

- Satan's world says that personal peace can be found with financial security.

- Satan's world says that sex should not be restricted to marriage.

- Satan's world says the most important thing in life is to feel good about yourself..

Satan's world is not what it seems. You must prepare your children for a world which is deceptive by its very nature. For the most part, the people in this world do not realize they are being deceived. Most would be shocked and horrified to know that they actually are serving Satan. College professors, business executives, country music groups, self-help gurus, rock groups, movie actors and others who do not know Christ are, in fact, serving the cause of Satan, whether they realize it or not. People who think they have the answers to life are, in fact, being led down a path of deception that will one day eventually end in great sadness and horror.

Ask David.

You, too, can be deceived. Just ask David.

The Bible records an example of Satan's dangerous deception in the form of a story about King David. The example is not a single incident, it is a single moment of deception with epic consequences. Because of David's exemplary behavior prior to this incident, and the clear trail of devastation that follows, it is a dramatic story for teaching your children about deception. This story is about the same David who killed Goliath; who maintained integrity and loyalty to King Saul while fleeing from him; who successfully fought God's enemies for Israel; who brought the ark of the covenant back to the tabernacle and who was "a man after God's own heart." If this same David could be deceived by the world and fall into grievous sin, anyone can, including your child. The heartbreaking consequences are spelled out clearly. Your child can understand them and remember them as an example and a warning.

You probably know the story already. David was king of Israel. His army had gone to war. One night, from his rooftop, he saw Bathsheba bathing. He had several wives already, but they were not enough. He watched Bathsheba and was attracted to her. He was deceived; he thought he could satisfy his desire secretly, without serious consequences. The attraction led quickly to sin and spiraled into a dark nightmare of consequences. After the guilt of adultery, David arranged the murder of a brave soldier to cover up his sin. In order to accomplish that, David became indebted to Joab, the unscrupulous, opportunistic general who arranged for Uriah's death in battle. Then David and Bathsheba's baby had to die. Later, David's sin caused him to turn a blind eye to his son Amnon's rape of his half-sister, Tamar. David's failure to punish Amnon enraged Absalom, Tamar's full brother. Absalom's anger festered for a time until it broke out in revenge. He murdered Amnon and, eventually, attempted to usurp the throne from his father. Finally, Absalom was slain by Joab (against David's orders) as he hung from the branch of a tree, caught by his long and beautiful hair. David's grief was overwhelming.

Do you think that if David had realized all the consequences that would follow his lustful glance at Bathsheba he would have pursued his course of adultery? No, of course not. How many times have you said (along with David), "if only I had known"? Yet this is what the way of the wicked is like. This is the message that you are to tell your children. *If you, as a Christian, choose to take this road, you will be deceived, just as David was.*

David thought only for the moment. He thought only of the physical allure of the woman he saw. He acted on the basis of his feelings rather than on the basis of what God wanted him to do. He chose the way of the wicked over the way of the righteous. This is why Proverbs 4:15 shouts, **"Avoid it, do not travel on it; turn from it and go on your way."**

Sadly, David did not go on his way. Look at the path of destruction, sorrow, agony and heartbreak that followed. Another of his sons, King Solomon, witnessed the devastation in his family throughout his childhood and youth. That was likely at least part of the impetus driving him when he wrote his proverbs. Proverbs 4 is an eloquent, passionate plea for children to heed the wisdom

and warnings of their parents. Read the chapter with the context
of Solomon's sad family history in mind. Hear his intensity.

> Listen, my sons, to a father's instruction;
> pay attention and gain understanding.
> I give you sound learning,
> so do not forsake my teaching.
> When I was a boy in my father's house,
> still tender, and an only child of my mother,
> he taught me and said,
> "Lay hold of my words with all your heart;
> keep my commands and you will live.
> Get wisdom, get understanding;
> do not forget my words or swerve from them.
> Do not forsake wisdom, and she will protect you;
> love her, and she will watch over you.
> Wisdom is supreme; therefore get wisdom.
> Though it cost all you have, get understanding.
> Esteem her, and she will exalt you;
> embrace her, and she will honor you.
> She will set a garland of grace on your head
> and present you with a crown of splendor."

> Listen, my son, accept what I say,
> and the years of your life will be many.
> I guide you in the way of wisdom
> and lead you along straight paths.
> When you walk, your steps will not be hampered;
> when you run, you will not stumble.
> Hold on to instruction, do not let it go;
> guard it well, for it is your life.
> Do not set foot on the path of the wicked

or walk in the way of evil men.

Avoid it, do not travel on it;

turn from it and go on your way.

For they cannot sleep till they do evil;

they are robbed of slumber till they make someone fall.

They eat the bread of wickedness

and drink the wine of violence.

The path of the righteous is like the first gleam of dawn,

shining ever brighter till the full light of day.

But the way of the wicked is like deep darkness;

they do not know what makes them stumble.

My son, pay attention to what I say;

listen closely to my words.

Do not let them out of your sight,

keep them within your heart;

for they are life to those who find them

and health to a man's whole body.

Above all else, guard your heart,

for it is the wellspring of life.

Put away perversity from your mouth;

keep corrupt talk far from your lips.

Let your eyes look straight ahead,

fix your gaze directly before you.

Make level paths for your feet

and take only ways that are firm.

Do not swerve to the right or the left;

keep your foot from evil.

Bring this passion to your children, in your greenhouse, when you warn them not to set foot on the path of the wicked. Teach your children to see life from God's perspective. God says the way of the righteous is good. It will bring peace and protection. God says the way of the wicked is deceitful and dangerous and stupid.

The world, the deceptive way of the wicked, says, "Go ahead, look, enjoy! What harm is there in seeing a beautiful woman? What harm is there in having the *Sports Illustrated* Swimsuit Calendar hanging in your room or office? What harm is there in being a red-blooded American male who admires a young woman's body?

What harm is there? Don't be deceived. Ask David. What harm is there in dressing in such a way that your body attracts attention? What harm is there? Ask Bathsheba.

Christians are subjects in the kingdom of God, not the kingdom of this world.

You must teach your children to see the total difference between these two kingdoms. Satan wants to minimize or deny the differences. He wants you off your guard. If your children don't see the dangers, they are vulnerable to the world's deceptive allure.

You hear and see the lies all the time. I listed some of them earlier in this chapter. You already recognize many of them and guard your children from them. But you can never let your guard down; the danger comes from the lies you aren't aware of, the ones you have overlooked! What can you do about them? God gave you the tools to detect and expose the lies of the world.

The greatest tool is the Bible itself. The Word is truth and light, and it exposes lies and darkness. The more you study and use the Bible, the more discerning you become about the world. Watch what goes on in the world and ask yourself questions. Ask if what the world says is really true.

For example, entertainment is often based on the humorous portrayal of lust, adultery, jealousy, gossip, hatred, greed, etc. I'm not just talking about X-rated movies; light-hearted, fun PG movies fit the profile just as well. Why do we find it so easy to be amused by behavior that God hates and that Jesus Christ died to save us from? Is there, perhaps, some kind of deception going on that says, "It's no big deal, it's just fun"?

Another popular lie is that sensual pleasure satisfies. We aren't fooled by that lie, are we? Even non-Christians warn their children against the deadly pleasures of drugs, alcohol and promiscuous sex. But how about the more wholesome pleasures? Food, recreation, music, travel, cars, computers—these can all provide legitimate enjoyment. But one of the world's lies is that worldly pleasure itself is worth living for. Just watch commercials for an evening. The only issue is to decide what product or experience gives the greatest pleasure. When your children beg for the newest action figure, video game, or CD; when you find yourself craving a faster car, a more luxurious vacation, a more powerful computer, a better wardrobe—stop and check yourself. None of those things is necessarily wrong, but will any of them really bring the satisfaction they promise?

You must tell your children over and over that satisfaction and contentment are impossible apart from a right relationship with God. Satan wants people to think he can offer more pleasure than God can. That's a lie. The world's "pleasures" don't deliver what they promise, and what enjoyment they do bring doesn't last. A Christian, however, can find contentment and satisfaction in any situation; and only a Christian can fully enjoy all the pleasures mentioned above, because he doesn't depend on them for happiness. He can take or leave them because he finds his joy in God.

Christians live in the world, but are not of the world. They are subjects in the kingdom of God. God's kingdom is the only place of genuine truth and strength and beauty. Talk to your children about Satan's deception. Teach them not to be deceived by the world. Teach them not to trade the truth of God for the lies of Satan.

Application Questions

1. What are some lies from the entertainment world that might appeal to your children?

2. What are some lies that might be told to your children from the educational system?

3. Describe how you would explain to your children that the world can be attractive and, at the same time, dangerous and deceitful.

Footnotes

[1] Jay Adams, *Christian Living in the World,* (Woodruff, SC: Timeless Texts, 1998) p. 33-35.

[2] Laura Branigan, *Self Control* (Atlantic Recording Corporation, 1984)

Everyday Talk about Sex

In the last chapter we saw that satan is engaged in deceiving the world. As we found out in the story of King David, sexual temptation is an area in which Satan has been particularly successful. In the era of cable TV it seems almost absurd to turn to God and His Bible to understand sex. The idea that sex is God's creation and gift to man does not compute in the 21st century world. The Great Deceiver has been hard at work. Good sex is portrayed as naughty sex. To be good in bed is to be bad in bed. Chastity, purity and modesty are no longer considered virtues. Instead of being marks of honor these qualities have become indicators of a damaged psyche. This is the everyday talk that your child hears about sex from friends, movies, TV and the classroom. Conventional wisdom says the world, not God, has the answers about sex.

Pornography has made its way from adult bookstores and movie houses found in the "bad parts of town" to your living room. Cable and satellite TV networks and otherwise first class hotels offer pornography without shame.

The Holy Spirit gave the Apostle Paul the same concerns

that He gave Solomon. Paul puts it this way in Ephesians 4:17-19:

> So I tell you this, and insist on it in the Lord, that you
> must no longer live as the Gentiles do, in the futility
> of their thinking. They are darkened in their under-
> standing and separated from the life of God because of
> the ignorance that is in them due to the hardening of
> their hearts. Having lost all sensitivity, they have given
> themselves over to sensuality so as to indulge in every
> kind of impurity, with a continual lust for more.

Paul says that the world has it all wrong. Sensuality is not sensitivity. Paul says bluntly: don't think like the world. Read his words of warning. The Gentiles (that is, the world apart from God's people) do not understand. Their thinking is clouded and dark and separated from the life of God. Paul emphasized sensuality as a prime example of the world's polluted thinking. This word *sensuality* is also listed by Paul as one of the deeds of the flesh in Gal. 5:19. *The Linguistic Key to the Greek New Testament* defines the Greek word for sensuality this way: " . . . unrestrained living, unbridled acts of indecency which shock the public."[1]

From a biblical perspective, sex requires great sensitivity. The focus of biblical sex is on how to please your marriage compan-ion. Notice the stark contrast with the world's understanding of sexuality. Unrestrained lust is the world's ideal for sex. And certainly, any trip to the movie theatre, video store or TV set will quickly confirm the influence of the world. Sex is portrayed as a recreational activity that all are entitled to in any form desired. This understanding of sex does not cultivate sensitivity; it only brings a continual thirst for more and more indulgence of the flesh.

God wants you to talk to your children about this deception. The reason that your everyday talk must include sex is that they are exposed to the world's false view of sex. As we established in the last chapter, your child is already hearing Satan's deceitful version of sex from the world. Remember that *Empower America's* statistics indicate that the average preschooler watches twenty-eight hours of television each week. The average teenager watches twenty-one hours of television each week. Try watching twenty-eight hours of television during a given week and see whether sex is a part of the electronic milieu. If your children attend movies, what sort of things will they see? Will there be discussion and depiction of sexuality in these movies? What about the previews of upcoming movies played before the main feature film? Is sex a part of the entertainment culture of your world? Of course it is. Do children, young or old, talk about what they see on TV or in the movies? The answer, of course, is yes.

Even if your child never sees any television or movies, he will still be exposed to the world's concept of sexuality. He will hear it from the children that he plays with. Talk about sex is a part of every school situation. Suppose you attempt to cut your child completely off from the world? As unwise as that would be, there will still be contact. There is more than enough information in the form of short comments, quotations in books, pictures on billboards, stories and pictures in magazines and catalogs to influence your child's concept of sex. Whether you like or admit it, your child is hearing from the world about sex. That is why God wants you to talk to your children about it. Your children need to hear in your everyday talk what God says and thinks about sexuality. You need to prepare your kids for Satan's lies and deceptions about sex. Your children need to know that sensitivity and sensuality are two very different, indeed, opposite things.

How do you begin this conversation? Take comfort that you don't have to begin talking about sex the way the world does. Graphic content and biological illustrations are not profitable for discussion about sex with your very young children. It is better to keep it simple and conceptual in the beginning.

Tell them something like this:

"Sex is something special that God created for married people. It is a way for mommies and daddies to be close and special with each other. Sex is a blessing because it is designed to help husbands and wives know each other and bring joy to each other. Sex is also how God makes babies grow inside of mommies. But, sometimes people who aren't married want to be close like that, and that is bad."

Initially that is all that you need to say. Learn how to communicate these thoughts to your children in your own words.

As time passes and your children grow older you will tell them more, as they are ready. Proverbs 7 will help your children see reality from God's perspective. Be sure to teach them this perspective well before they encounter sexual temptation themselves. A six- or seven-year-old will probably be more receptive to this conversation than a sixteen-year-old! God has not left you without powerful resources in His Word. But you must use them. You must use these powerful weapons in your everyday talk.

Remember these basic facts:

- The world is deceptive
- The flesh is deceptive
- The Devil is deceptive

His own flesh deceived David. He believed the lies of lust. He thought only of immediate pleasure, never thinking it would destroy those things he loved most. What about the world you and your children live in? Is this world any less deceptive than David's? Only someone living in a palace that overlooked the homes of Jerusalem could have seen a woman bathing on a rooftop. Today, these glimpses and much more are available to all, rich or poor. Billboards on the way to church, TV commercials, movie previews, magazines, popular music videos and catalogs offer many such glimpses designed to tempt the flesh to acts of lust.

Remember, all it took was one occasion to fuel the fires of lust that brought such agony to a godly man like David and such dishonor to God's Name. Do you think that you and your children can remain unscathed by the constant, prolonged portrayal of lust and sensuality by the twenty-first century entertainment industry? Are you godlier than David?

Like it or not, lust has forced its ugly head into our daily lives. Sensuality is a part of your daily life. It is a part of your child's daily life. This intrusion is, at its root, deceptive. It says that sex the world's way is not so bad. The illusion says lust is good and natural, as long as you don't overdo it. Sex outside of marriage is condoned by our society as an essential part of relationships outside of marriage. Living together is no longer a scandal. Marital infidelity is no longer a flaw that should disqualify someone from public office, even the highest one. Sex, lust and sensuality are okay for America, okay for the world, okay for you, okay for your kids—just don't overdo it.

"NO, THEY ARE NOT!!" I hope you are shouting those words right now. God wants you to teach your children that lust and sensuality are wrong, and that sex outside of marriage is wrong. But it is not enough to teach them that it is wrong.

You must teach them how to guard against the temptations that will assault them. They must be warned about the weakness of their own flesh. You have to tell them that when the temptation comes, sex won't seem bad, it will seem like the most wonderful experience they have ever had—until it's too late.

Here is an example that illustrates the deceptive schemes that await your children.

Kate was a good Christian girl from a strong home. During high school she had friends in her church youth group, but never dated. In college, when no relationships with guys ever seemed to develop, she naturally wondered what was wrong with her. Finally she met Bruce, a mature, respected, popular Christian young man. They fell in love and were soon engaged to be married. But suddenly he broke off the engagement, explaining that his feelings for her just weren't strong enough for marriage. Kate felt devastated. After weeks of lonely misery, with no one else to turn to, she went to her pastor. "Why is this happening?" she asked. "Is it me? What's wrong with me? Who can help me understand? I don't know what to do!"

The pastor encouraged her kindly. Finding a sympathetic listener, she returned and talked further with him. One day, suddenly, the conversation became inappropriately personal. At first Kate was startled and quickly left the meeting, but as she thought about it further, the warmth and intimacy of the conversation seemed irresistible. She stifled her conscience and went back for more. "Maybe I'm just too cautious," she reasoned, "maybe my whole problem is all about being too timid. After all, he is my pastor, and he's just trying to help me grow in this area. What harm can there be, really?"

Sadly, she found out. Thinking she was strong, she was deceived by the weakness of her own flesh. All of a sudden, she gave in to the promise of intimacy, and she found out that the

power of sexual sin is a cruel trap to escape from. She found out
that she wasn't as "good" as she thought she was. Kate did not
flee temptation; she reasoned with it, and gave in to it.

Proverbs 7 is a powerful tool. If Kate had had its message
impressed on her, it might have protected her. It illustrates the
stark difference between sensitivity and sensuality, between sex
that pleases God and sex that brings death. Notice the vivid
description in these verses. While the context is different, the
allure and deceit of sexual temptation are much the same as in
Kate's situation:

> She threw her arms around him and kissed him, and with
> a brazen look she said, "I've offered my sacrifices and just
> finished my vows. It's you I was looking for! I came out to
> find you, and here you are! My bed is spread with colored
> sheets of finest linen imported from Egypt. I've perfumed
> my bed with myrrh, aloes, and cinnamon. Come, let's
> drink our fill of love until morning. Let's enjoy each
> other's caresses, for my husband is not home. He's away
> on a long trip. He has taken a wallet full of money with
> him, and he won't return until later in the month.
>
> So she seduced him with her pretty speech. With her
> flattery she enticed him. He followed her all at once, like
> an ox going to the slaughter or like a trapped stag, await-
> ing the arrow that would pierce its heart. He was like a
> bird flying into a snare, little knowing it would cost him
> his life.
>
> Listen to me, my sons, and pay attention to my words.
> Don't let your hearts stray away toward her. Don't
> wander down her wayward path. For she has been the

ruin of many; numerous men have been her victims. Her
house is the road to the grave. Her bedroom is the den of
death. (Proverbs 7:13-20 NLT)

These verses illustrate the deceit of sexual temptation. Holly-
wood could not have crafted a more appealing scene. Everything
was set for a time of pleasure and passion. The woman was
dressed to seduce. Religious obligations had been met. The
bed was attractive. The husband was gone. Why not have
some pleasure? Why not enjoy the blessings of sex? Viewed by
themselves, verses 13-20 are persuasive. That is how deception
is presented to your children by the world. The deception is that
sexual sin appears to be the most desirable thing at the moment.
That is why your children need to visualize the scene of Proverbs
7 long before temptation comes to them so they can recognize it
when they see it.

The lifestyle of this lustful woman was well known. She
never stayed at home. She or one of her sisters was always on the
corner offering sex to any who would take it. Yet the young man
believed her lie that she was out looking only for him.

Verse 21 brings you back to stark reality. The attractive
scene was only an illusion. The young man was enticed, trapped,
flattered and led like an ox to the slaughter. Her bedroom was
a bedroom of death. She offered not sex, but lust; not pleasure,
but torment.

So here in Proverbs, a book designed for the instruction of
the young in the ways of God, lies this graphic description of the
power of sexual lust and sin. Do you dare give your children any
less than the warning God provides? Do you want your son or
daughter to blunder into the trap of sexual temptation with the
self-centered naivete of a girl like Kate or the foolishness of the
young man in Proverbs 7?

Chapter 7 is a wonderful example of the power of everyday talk. It not only gives you the illustration, it shows you how to teach it to your children. Look at the way the father began the illustration:

> I was looking out the window of my house one day and saw a simpleminded young man who lacked common sense. He was crossing the street near the house of an immoral woman. He was strolling down the path by her house at twilight, as the day was fading, as the dark of night set in. The woman approached him, dressed seductively and sly of heart. She was the brash, rebellious type who never stays at home. She is often seen in the streets and markets, soliciting at every corner. (Proverbs 7:6-12 NLT)

In verses six through twelve the father (or mother) made use of something that he had seen right from his own window. Everyday talk corresponds to everyday life. This parent did not shrink back from the opportunity to tell it like it is. The allure of lust was not denied. However, neither were the horrible consequences minimized.

You too have these opportunities—daily! Scenes on TV and in movies, as well as events in real life, closely resemble the setting in Proverbs 7. You see events, perhaps even through your own living room window, that offer you the same opportunity to talk about sex. If you do not tell your children that lust is not biblical sex, you will leave them to be prey for the hunter's snare that Proverbs 7 describes. That is exactly what Moses meant in Deuteronomy 6. Along the path of everyday life, take the opportunities that God gives you to instruct your children.

This father was deeply concerned that his children not fall

prey to the deception of lust. Notice the powerful plea he makes at the beginning of the chapter.

> Follow my advice, my son; always treasure my commands. Obey them and live! Guard my teachings as your most precious possession. Tie them on your fingers as a reminder. Write them deep within your heart. Love wisdom like a sister; make insight a beloved member of your family. Let them hold you back from an affair with an immoral woman, from listening to the flattery of an adulterous woman. (Proverbs 7:1-5 NLT)

These words require tremendous courage for you as a parent to speak. These words expose your own sin and vulnerability. They cut deeply. Who are you, and who am I, to say these words? Parent, if you have come with me this far, come with me a little farther. Look at verse one.

"Follow my advice, my son; always treasure my commands."

Doesn't this sound arrogant? "Always treasure my commands." Why should my children, who see my daily struggle with my own sins, treasure my commands? As your children grow older, one painful fact becomes clearer each day: they become more aware of your sins. Parents, just as King David failed to punish his son for the sin of which he himself was also guilty, our own sin tends to keep us from embracing the power of the words in verse one. How can we, who fail so often and so badly, expect our children to treasure our instruction?

You must believe with all your heart that God holds the key to life in His Word. You must believe this so deeply that two things must happen. First, you must tell them the truth the way Solomon does here—not because you are the standard, but because God's Word is true whether you have followed it or not.

Second, you must believe this so genuinely that you change your own ways where you are failing, repent and embrace the sanctifying truth of God.

The next two verses continue this theme: "Obey them and live! Guard my teachings as your most precious possession. Tie them on your fingers as a reminder. Write them deep within your heart" (Proverbs 7:2–3 NLT).

Do your children regard your teaching as their most precious possession? God wants your words about Him to sink deep into the hearts of your children. Again, I look at my own sin and failure and I shrink back. Yet God wants you and me to bring His truth to our children with such love that it will etch itself into their hearts. Where we have failed, our children need to hear of our repentance and of God's forgiveness. They need to see that our own failings will not keep us from teaching what is of true value in this world.

Parents, your children should hear God's truth from your lips. Yes, it is important for them to hear it from the pastor and from others. But your children must also hear it from you. They must hear God's truth in your everyday talk. You must look out the window to your world and talk to your children about the truth of God in relation to what you see. If you want your children to withstand the onslaught of sensuality into their lives, you must give them the precious treasure of frank, honest, everyday talk about sexual temptation. This is the point of verses 4-5 of chapter seven: "Love wisdom like a sister; make insight a beloved member of your family. Let them hold you back from an affair with an immoral woman, from listening to the flattery of an adulterous woman."

In these verses the Holy Spirit urges the love of wisdom and insight.

The Spirit depicts a close, intimate relationship with God's Word as taught by the parents. This relationship with the Word is alive and vital. Thus, this combination of treasuring the commands of parents and loving the wisdom and insight of God upon which these commands are based provides protection from the immoral woman.[2] A strong relationship with parents, along with wisdom and insight from God's Word, forms the barriers of protection that help your children resist the temptation to lust.

It is mandatory that you talk with your children about the truth taught in Proverbs 7:1-5. If necessary, present your kids with the dilemma the passages present to you as a parent. You know that you are not perfect. So do your children. You know that your parenting style doesn't always encourage your children to accept your words as precious treasure. Talk with your children about how you can both get to where God wants you to be. Can this process be difficult and painful? Yes, it can be. But over time by God's grace, genuine progress will occur. This requires faith. But, praise God, He is faithful!

Sexual temptation and sexual perversion are such a common, pervasive presence in our day that we must teach our children about purity from their earliest years. While it seems intimidating to many, it is not really a very complicated topic. As we have seen, the Bible gives you plenty of material to use in your instruction. The most effective strategy is to include it in your everyday talk.

Application Questions

1. At what age do children typically see or hear about sexual sin? At what age should your children receive your instruction about sexual sin?

2. List several examples of sexual misconduct that your
    children might see, such as on TV programs or advertis-
    ing. How can your everyday talk about such behavior train
    them to be pure?

3. What safeguards can you realistically provide to protect
    your children from unnecessary sexual temptation?

4. Consider how the world's view of sex has influenced your
    own view. How do your own views need to change in
    order to think more biblically about sex?

Footnotes

[1] Fritz Reineker and Cleon Rogers, *The Linguistic Key to the Greek New
    Testament* (Grand Rapids: ZondervanPublishing House, 1980), page
    517.

[2] The passage does not intend to say that only immoral women can be a
    danger. Daughters will be protected from immoral men as well by
    following the same directives.

Eleven

Everyday Talk about Music

If any subject is more difficult to discuss with your children than sex, it just might be music, contemporary music. Let me begin with a story from my own youth.

In 1963, I was on the high school football team. My parents were strong Christians and concerned about the impact of the world upon their children. As the saying goes, I didn't get out much. One day in the locker room after practice a senior asked me what I thought of the Beach Boys' hit tune, "Be True to Your School." For those of you not familiar with ancient history, the Beach Boys were a collection of bleached-blond slightly hung-over surfers who sang about big waves, fast cars, California girls and parties. In the early sixties these sorts of themes appealed to kids. In any event, I answered that I had never heard of the song. The response from this senior "star" player was stunned aston-ishment. He assumed that everybody had heard this song. He looked at me with a mixture of pity, amazement and unbelief. I was definitely "not with it." The impact was devastating. I was clearly out of touch with the world around me. I was not cool.

This illustration shows that music matters in the lives of

young people. Because music matters to teenagers, it matters to younger children as well. Kids are not interested in being social outcasts.

In the everyday world, music matters. Music award shows multiply. We have the Grammy awards, the Dove Awards, The American Music Awards, the Gospel Music Awards, The Country Music Awards, The MTV Awards, The Rap Music Awards and on and on and on. In 1999, Americans spent $14.6 billion dollars on music purchases. Music is big business in America. Actually, music is a big deal in almost all cultures and communities of the world. Why? Because God made music to be important.

Obviously, music has a powerful impact upon people. We tend to think of the dominance of music as a recent trend introduced by modern recording technology. However, read this account of a young and popular musician.

> He was as concerned about the way he appeared when he
> performed as the music he played . . . Around him young
> women swooned, others fought for and tore articles of
> his clothing . . . The musician encouraged such conduct
> because it made his
> legend grow.[1]

Who was this wild man after whom young women clamored? Is this a scene from the 90's, 80's, 70's or 60's? Actually, it is from the 30's—the 1830's. The musician was Franz Liszt, the noted classical pianist and composer. No, he wasn't the first rock musician. His concert music was the same music that can still be heard on public radio during their classical hours. His music is neither loud nor raucous by our standards. It is not performed by strange-looking musicians whose photos give parents nightmares. Liszt produced the same reactions in his listeners as did Elvis and the Beatles. Music is powerful. Because it is powerful, we must understand the source and purpose of music.

The Bible gives insight about the power of music. We know from Revelation 5:9 and from the announcement of the birth of Christ and other passages that music is an act of worship that goes on in heaven. This tells us that music is of heavenly origin. Music existed before man was created. Anything that was used in heaven to honor God before the earth was created has great power and significance.

God's purpose for music here on earth is to strengthen and intensify our relationship with him.

Do not miss the importance of this point when you think or talk about music. Music is not the invention of man, but of God. Music is designed first and foremost to praise God. Listen to the words of Psalm 92:1-4:

> It is good to praise the LORD
> and make music to your name, O Most High,
> to proclaim your love in the morning
> and your faithfulness at night,
> to the music of the ten-stringed lyre
> and the melody of the harp.
>
> For you make me glad by your deeds, O LORD;
> I sing for joy at the works of your hands.

The Psalmist says it is a good thing to make music and praise God. Music can have the power to focus your mind on the glory of God. Music can stimulate joy and gratitude. Music has the potential to direct your mind toward meditation on God and His ways. Music can help create a deep, emotional, relational loyalty toward God. And as we shall see in a moment, music used without God as its focus can also help foster deep, emotional, relational loyalties toward God's enemies.

How does the Bible illustrate the good effects of music on your relationship with God? First, music expressed love and loyalty for God's truth. After God dramatically rescued Israel from Egypt, Moses led the Israelites in a song to celebrate the power of God's redemption. To help Israel remember the great power of the faithfulness of God, Moses provided a song for Israel to use to keep the great redemptive act close and clear in their thinking.

> And when the Israelites saw the great power the LORD
> displayed against the Egyptians, the people feared the
> LORD and put their trust in him and in Moses his
> servant. Then Moses and the Israelites sang this song to
> the LORD:
>
> "I will sing to the LORD,
> for he is highly exalted.
> The horse and its rider
> he has hurled into the sea.
>
> The LORD is my strength and my song;
> he has become my salvation." (Exodus 14:31–15:2)

Second, Moses provided a song for Israel to remember the great redemptive acts of God in the history of Israel. As they prepared to enter the Promised Land, he reminded them of God's covenant relationship with them in the song recorded in

Deuteronomy 31:30.

Third, music can bring calmness as we see when David sang his songs to sooth the tormented spirit of King Saul. The psalms are alive with the power and beauty of music.

Fourth, in Colossians 3:16, Paul mentions the use of music "in your heart" to keep Christians focused on priorities that please God.

However, in a similar way, music has the potential to help establish wickedness as a lifestyle.

In Exodus 32:18, "Moses replied: 'It is not the sound of victory, it is not the sound of defeat; it is the sound of singing that I hear.'"

This shows that Israel was again using music to establish and exult in a commitment they had made. But unlike the joy and praise of God that was the focus of the song in Exodus 15, this time the commitment was to wickedness and disobedience. Music was used to celebrate the sinful actions of Israel just as music had earlier been used to celebrate the faithfulness of God. The people sang and danced around the image of a golden calf. This was the awful sound that Moses heard as he came down from the mountain. Similar uses of music to support wickedness are demonstrated in Amos 5:21-24 and Ezekiel 26:13.

We see that people use music to enhance both righteous and wicked behaviors. This is just like James' warning about the use of your tongue. The same mouth can both praise and blaspheme. Obviously, music itself is not the problem. Nothing indicates that the style of music was the issue. Rather, if the heart is right, music can establish that goodness and encourage more goodness and growth. But if the heart is not focused on the praise of God, then music can hasten the slide down the path of sin and destruction. People allow themselves to be swayed by the power of the music, and when the attitudes and emotions are negative, the music can lead to relational loyalties far away from God.

The only setting in which music will accomplish good rather than evil is in a life that is controlled by the Spirit's Word and a heart that wants to sing God's praises.

> And do not get drunk with wine, for that is dissipation,
> but be filled with the Spirit, speaking to one another
> in psalms and hymns and spiritual songs, singing and
> making melody with your heart to the Lord; always giving
> thanks for all things in the name of our Lord Jesus Christ
> to God, even the Father . . . . (Ephesians 5:18-20 NASB)

Ephesians 5:19 says there is a song that God wants playing in your heart and in your children's hearts. The apostle Paul talks about "singing and making melody with your heart to the Lord" in the context of being filled with the Spirit and expressing gratitude to God. Whose song is playing in your heart? Is it the song of righteousness or the song of destruction? Is it the song of God or the song of the ruler of this world? That is the issue. Music, like anything else in this world, is not neutral. It will either enhance your relationship with God or draw you away from Him and toward the world. Jesus said, "He who is not with me is against me."

You want your children to be conscious of the raw power of music. Music is one of the things that is in this world and is also in the world to come. Music is powerful. It will either enhance your relationship (or your children's) with God or it will enhance your relationship with someone or something else. When Satan fell from heaven he must have carried his memories of music with him. As we have noted, Satan is first and foremost the great deceiver, and he is clever. Music has become a powerful tool in his deception.

Let's take a brief look at how music can be negative. Early in her history, Israel knew that she was disobeying God when she made the golden calves. Music helped her follow through with her sin. Many years later, when God (through Amos) accused Israel of hypocrisy in worship, He specifically rejected their music:

> I hate, I despise your religious feasts;
> I cannot stand your assemblies.
> Even though you bring me burnt offerings and grain
>   offerings,
> I will not accept them.
> Though you bring choice fellowship offerings,
> I will have no regard for them.
> Away with the noise of your songs!
> I will not listen to the music of your harps.
> But let justice roll on like a river,
> righteousness like a never-failing stream! (Amos 5:21-24)

What music did God reject? The very psalms that He Himself had ordained for worship. This is profound! Pleasing God with music is first and foremost a matter of the heart. This passage ends the debate about which forms of music are good and which are bad. There is no question that the music in question was of good origin. The music came from God. Yet Israel used this wonderful music for her own ends. So, instead of building a closer relationship with God, it became a tool of estrangement from Him.

Music, then, is designed to enhance relationships. Parents, you must get this. If you attempt to control your children's music without understanding its relational impact you will not be able to have productive everyday talk with your kids. Instead, you will alienate them.

When your child discovers music that he loves, music that he listens to over and over, something in that music is resonating with him. The music somehow expresses what he feels, or verbalizes his thoughts and attitudes. He invests himself in the songs or in the performers and becomes attached to them. If you threaten to take away his music because you don't approve of it, you may be threatening him personally in a way you are not even aware of. Granted, you can see that this "relationship" is one-sided, illusory and negative, but if he perceives it to be a source of deep satisfaction, he will likely resent your "interference."

If you become locked in a debate with your kids about the forms of music, you will eventually lose the debate. If you debate about whether rock or country or classical or folk or jazz or R&B or fusion or any other form is good or bad, you will miss the point. You will miss the opportunity to help your kids understand the power of music to build their relationship with God. The problem with the music that God detested in Amos 5 was not the form of the music, but the attitude of the heart. The simple requirement of godly music is that it must be used to point to God.

Beethoven was a godless man bent upon the praise of man, as his Ninth Symphony, with its "Ode to Joy," illustrates. Yet his music resonates with beauty and power. It is possible to listen to his music and praise God in your heart or, conversely, to honor man in your heart. It is a matter of the orientation of your heart. Rock music, by itself, does not have to be anti-God, although much of it is ungodly. The issue again is a matter of the heart.

Does this mean that the form of music is irrelevant? No. But the important point is that the form or style of music is not the issue. If psalms written by the Holy Spirit can be sung in such a way that God rejects them, then we must conclude that God is interested in more than form. Much contemporary music rightly disturbs because it is used to promote evil. However, it is possible that these same forms can be used to praise God.

One example is the music of Rich Mullins. He used contemporary forms to carry a God-centered message. His lyrics are thoughtful, profound and humble, and full of exuberant praise to God. In one of his songs (that turned out to be humanly prophetic) he says,

> I'll keep rocking till I am sure it is my time to roll.
> When I leave I want to go out like Elijah. ...
>
> It won't break my heart to say goodbye.

Mullins echoes Paul's words in Philippians 1:21, "For to me, to live is Christ and to die is gain." NASB

This book is not the place to launch into a full discussion of music and its impact upon your relationship with God. However, if you are able to have everyday talk with your children in which the discussion centers on how music enhances or weakens their relationship with God, you will have won a major victory.

Music can tempt your child to see himself as an outsider and an outcast. During the teenage years many young people struggle with uncertainty, insecurity, self-pity and other emotional ups and downs. Popular songs often put words to the very issues kids are experiencing. Negative emotions of self-pity and despair can be intensified. Music can subtly influence your child to identify with those who hate God. That is the danger you must teach them to avoid. But music used for the glory of God can also help your child identify with God and His people. That is where your everyday talk should focus.

Whose music is playing in your children's heart? Whose music is playing in your heart?

Application Questions

1. What role does music play in people's lives?

2. What defines music as good or bad? What is the potential negative impact of bad music?

3. What is the potential positive impact of good music?

4. What should be the focus of your everyday talk about music?

You Are on Display

With chapter 12 you are almost to the end of the book. It is time to return to the theme of the first chapter—that your everyday talk is your most important weapon in the great spiritual battle to lead your kids to new life in Christ. Your everyday talk models attitudes and behavior to your children. They learn not only from your everyday talk to them, but from your everyday talk to others. Just as your casual, unguarded everyday talk with your children effectively influences them, your casual, unguarded everyday talk with your spouse and others—that your children observe—also influences them.

Recall the themes of the earlier chapters with me. How much is your appreciation of the gospel a part of your day-to-day conversation with those around you? What kind of listener are you? Do you use pleasant words in your everyday talk with others? Are you ordinary or holy in the way you react when others hurt you? Do you have your own list of big sins that really set you off when you see them in others? Remember that the focus in Deuteronomy 6 is on Israel drawing near to God and having His commands impressed upon their hearts.

Hear, O Israel: The LORD our God, the LORD is one.
Love the LORD your God with all your heart and with
all your soul and with all your strength. These commandments that I give you today are to be upon your hearts.
Impress them on your children. Talk about them when
you sit at home and when you walk along the road, when
you lie down and when you get up. (Deuteronomy 6:4–7)

Against this backdrop let's consider two important areas:
1) talk between husband and wife and 2) swearing. These are
important areas in which your everyday talk reveals the habit
patterns of your heart. Poor habits in these areas will affect your
children, whether you are conscious of it or not.

Talk between husband and wife

How do you talk to your spouse in front of your children?
Do you make fun of him? Do you complain about her? Do you
insult each other? Do your children hear you argue incessantly?
Are irritation and smoldering anger common in your home? Or
do you deal with conflict by just ignoring each other? How do
you talk about your spouse to others?

The way you talk to or about your spouse is a model of
instruction for your children. Your conversation is a powerful
influence, either for good or for bad. Comments to and about
your spouse, made in your children's hearing, tell them about
your marriage. If you often speak of marriage as a pain, a risk, a
disaster or a trial, you are teaching your children what you think
marriage is really like. You are also displaying a view of marriage
that is contrary to God's view.

On the positive side, children also model your good, loving
behavior. Children whose parents are patient and kind to each

other tend to exhibit patient and kind behavior themselves. When Dad and Mom love to spend time talking together, when they are "best friends" who tell each other everything, the kids draw strength from this relationship and reflect the security and joy of a happy marriage.

Listen to yourself. Listen to the thoughts of your heart. What you say to yourself in your heart, the words that no one else hears except God—those inner words eventually see the light of day in your everyday talk. Listen to yourself speak to your family. Why? Because the biblical themes that we have addressed in this book must be woven into the fabric of your own life if you are to please God with your everyday talk. You can't teach what you don't have.

This is vital. You must be able to listen to yourself. If you have a hard time listening to yourself, ask your spouse to tell you what you say. I know that this may seem like a risky request. It may have painful results, but it is a request you need to make. You must become self-aware in this area. What kind of model are you? Do your children look forward to marriage? Do they want a marriage like yours? Remember that everyday talk is one of your most powerful teaching tools about marriage.

Marriage has fallen on hard times in the 21st century. *The Index of Leading Cultural Indicators* reports that in 2001, forty out of every one hundred first marriages ends in divorce, compared to sixteen out of every one hundred first marriages in 1960.[1] Many of you reading this have experienced divorce. It is vital that your everyday talk reflects God's perspective on marriage and not the world's view or your own sinful view, if it is not in line with God's.

When divorce is a part of your family history, your everyday talk must reflect God's healing power and your focus on serving Him now, rather than on the problems of a troubled past. This is the time to remember that Ephesians 4:29 says you must speak only what is useful to build up those who listen. If you are divorced, does your family hear that your former spouse is the cause of all your problems? Is your everyday talk filled with bitterness and hurt towards your former mate? Is that what you communicate to your kids? God is a God Who provides hope. He is the giver of all good things. Do not let a failed past marriage continue to do damage through your everyday talk. If your home is one of the increasing numbers of blended families, your focus and your everyday talk must be upon what God wants you to do now, not on the problems of the past.

Parents, listen to yourselves. Your children do. What do they hear? If things are difficult with your spouse, your everyday talk will reflect that reality. The two of you must understand the powerful message you are communicating to your children. Listen to yourself. This takes courage. Often your everyday talk is not pretty or productive. If this is the case, for the sake of God's honor and your children's wellbeing, your everyday talk must change.

How can your everyday talk change? This change will occur like all other biblical change—through repentance and faith. Repentance means that you will turn from your previous thoughts and practices and turn to God's good ways. Faith means that you follow God's way of talking, even when it hurts. Use your prayer times to cry out to God to help you change your everyday talk. Thankfully, God gives you specific instruction about what your everyday talk about others should be like. Recall the earlier chapters of this book and apply the principles you read there to your own everyday talk about your husband or wife. Think again about how Ephesians 4:29 applies to this aspect of your marriage.

Let no unwholesome word proceed from your mouth, but
only such a word as is good for edification according to
the need of the moment, so that it will give grace to those
who hear. (Ephesians 4:29 NASB)

You will recall that we looked at this verse in detail in
Chapter 7. Here is a summary of the verse as it applies specifically to everyday talk between husbands and wives.

First, Paul says that no unwholesome talk should come from
your mouth. What is unwholesome talk? Well, it can be many
things, but in this verse it means saying things that are not helpful
to others. These thirty-five words are among the most challenging in Scripture. The Holy Spirit is teaching you that words that
do not consider what is good for the hearer are unwholesome or
(as one translation says) rotten words. When you vent about your
spouse, your words are unwholesome. When you feel sorry for
yourself because of how wrong your spouse is, your words will
be unwholesome. When you do not think about how your words
will impact your children, your words are unwholesome.

Second, this passage teaches that you must be ready with
everyday talk that pleases God at a moment's notice. You must
be ready to respond to the need of the moment with everyday
talk that is specifically designed to benefit the person to whom
you are talking. This one phrase drives home the significance of
everyday talk like no other. You must be ready to respond with
helpful, building comments on the spur of the moment or your
everyday talk will be unwholesome, rotten talk.

Third, your focus must be upon giving help (grace) to your
hearer. In the context of everyday talk about your marriage, this
means that your words must seek to build up your spouse rather
than show disappointment, hurt, resentment or self-pity. That
is why you must listen to yourself. Take some time to talk with

your spouse. Ask for his or her forgiveness if your everyday talk has been unwholesome. Pray for change. Ask your spouse to help you change. If your children are old enough, ask them to help you change. If you tell your children they should obey God and follow Him while your everyday talk to and about your spouse is unwholesome, your training efforts will be counterproductive and your relationship with God will be frustrating to you. If your everyday talk is not consistent with God's direction in Deuteronomy 6, you will be at cross purposes with your heavenly Father. God wants you to trust Him in all things, including your everyday talk.

Swearing

Why swearing? Surely, even the world knows not to swear in front of children.

Perhaps this may be true for the moment. However, the growing reality is that swearing is fast becoming standard speech. Many modern dictionaries list vulgar words and their meanings. This acknowledges that swearing has become recognized as acceptable in everyday language. Swearing punctuates the everyday talk of the world. You hear it everywhere—at school, in the workplace, in movies and on TV, in books, sports, at parties and just about anywhere else. Swearing is how the world today gives expression and forcefulness to its conversation.

One of the first encounters a child will have with the world around him, as he takes exploratory ventures from your greenhouse, is with swearing. He will hear it on TV, from movies, from friends, he will hear it from sports stars and coaches and he will read various forms of expletives in best-selling books. Your child may even hear swearing from his family and friends at church.

As a teenager, I played on our church league softball team.

A certain preacher also played in the league. Whenever this preacher would strike out or hit a fly ball, we would hear a loud stream of profanity. The first few times we all thought it was coming from someone on the sidelines mocking him. Then someone finally realized the unthinkable: this stream of foul language was coming from the preacher. Everyday swearing—you can hear it anywhere.

Swearing is fast becoming one of the most blatant forms of hypocritical behavior. While it is still considered wrong for the President to swear during the State of the Union Address, numerous credible biographies of some Presidents suggest that they swear almost constantly when not on camera or in the public eye. As of this writing it is still politically incorrect to swear in front of young children, as this would set a bad example for the children. Yet our culture gives the distinct impression that to be a real man or real woman who really cares about issues, one must swear. No wonder adults often confuse children. A mark of the feminist liberation is that women are free to swear just as much as, if not more than, men. The reality is that swearing has become the emotional punctuation of modern speech.

There is danger in listening to the everyday talk of the world. Remember, 1 Corinthians 15:33 says, "Do not be deceived: 'Bad company corrupts good morals.'" Swearing is one of the corrupting elements that this verse warns about. Swearing attacks good character just as surely as acid attacks metal. At its root, swearing is proud, defiant language that scoffs at the holiness of God. Those who listen too much, too often, to the world, thinking they can handle it, are in peril of being corrupted. Like Lot pitching his tent toward Sodom, they gradually get comfortable living next to sin, tolerating it. The danger is not only in the actual swear words that are spoken; the danger is also in the attitude of arrogance, rebellion and rejection of God. Psalm 73:7-9 describes such people vividly:

> From their callous hearts comes iniquity;
> the evil conceits of their minds know no limits.
> They scoff, and speak with malice;
> in their arrogance they threaten oppression.
> Their mouths lay claim to heaven,
> and their tongues take possession of the earth.

Such people have no fear of God to restrain their speech. Their attitudes as well as their words can have a bad influence, even on Christians. This arrogant attitude is the danger hidden in swearing.

The world swears when it is ungrateful and angry at the way life unfolds. Anyone who thinks he deserves to have life unfold as he pleases is bound to be frustrated and discontent much of the time. People who don't get their own way in life begin to feel resentful and sorry for themselves. Self-pity is a powerful, negative attitude that gives rise to many, many excuses for sin. People fall into Satan's trap of giving themselves "permission" to sin to compensate for the difficulties and trials they've had to bear. Self-pity is a direct rejection of God's control. It is saying, "I don't like what you've done in my life, and I absolutely will not be content! I can't change it, so I'll just be angry and miserable." Thus, swearing is considered a justifiable response to unfair treatment. It is a way of letting others know that you have been wronged. This brand of self-pity is an ugly trait.

That is why it is dangerous for you to define the sin of swearing by a list of inappropriate four letter words. The real danger is that you will simply replace these unacceptable swear words with a list of words that are "okay" words that you may use instead. Let's look at Ephesians 5:4, in which Paul describes language that he says is unacceptable. "Nor should there be obscenity, foolish talk or coarse joking, which are out of place, but rather thanksgiving."

Ephesus was a cosmopolitan city, like many of our modern, major cities. Its people considered themselves sophisticated. The speech of the Ephesians had woven itself into the life of the church to the point where Paul had to address the issue specifically. Ephesians 5:4 contains an interesting *put off/put on* comparison. In the first part of the verse Paul directs that there should be no obscene, foolish talk. Again, he specifically states that there should not be any coarse jesting. *The Linguistic Key to the New Testament* provides some key definitions for these terms:

- **Obscene talk**—shameful, filthy or obscene speech

- **Foolish talk**—laughing at something without wit

- **Coarse jesting**—the word implies dexterity of turning a discourse to wit or humor, and lastly deceptive speech, so formed that the speaker easily contrives to wriggle of out its meaning or engagements. Ephesus was especially known for its facetious orators.[2]

The language Paul condemns is a broader category than what we generally define as swearing. The truth is, God has a higher standard for our speech than simply "not swearing." What does He want from us? Is it acceptable to use slang that substitutes euphemisms for profanity?

The "put on" response to swearing is gratitude. Notice the end of Ephesians 5:4. Paul says that gratitude should punctuate your speech, not swearing. This contrast is striking. It is not simply replacing one set of words with another set of words. God wants your grateful heart. He wants your faithful, trusting heart. He wants your submissive, humble heart. When He has these things from you, swearing will not be an issue. If your talk acknowledges that God has sovereign control over your life, and that He is working all things together for your good, you will express your gratitude, not your frustration or rebellion.

If your everyday talk is ungrateful and complaining, you are, in effect, swearing, even if you don't use swear words. The impact on your children will be the same. If, on the other hand, your everyday talk expresses gratitude and acceptance for God's Providence, you will have no need for the kind of language described in Ephesians 5:4. Both your words and your attitudes will honor God, not defy Him.

The point is that if you are not dominated by gratitude as Paul says you should be, then your attitude will mimic the world around you. You will unwittingly prepare your children to fall prey to the temptation of swearing and lack of gratitude. Without gratitude, there is no real defense against swearing or the ungrateful, self-pitying attitude that swearing represents. This is the message that Paul gave to the Ephesians. This is the message God wants you to give to your children.

You are on display.

These two areas of conversation, talk between husband and wife and the use of swearing, are not the whole picture. Consider for yourself other areas of your life where your everyday talk displays the attitude of your heart toward God. Deuteronomy 6:7 can be either a daunting, impossible command or it can be a joyful opportunity to express love and gratitude to the One who has rescued you from death and darkness and brought you into His blessed Kingdom of light.

Hear, O Israel: The LORD our God, the LORD is one.

Love the LORD your God with all your heart and with
all your soul and with all your strength. These commandments that I give you today are to be upon your hearts.
Impress them on your children. Talk about them when
you sit at home and when you walk along the road, when
you lie down and when you get up. (Deuteronomy 6:4-7)

Application Questions

1. Think about the everyday talk between you and your
   spouse. In what specific ways do you need to change?

2. What is the remedy if you have set a poor example of
   speech for your children? What is your hope?

3. How does swearing model a sinful *attitude* to your
   children?

4. List for yourself (if applicable) the specific language that
   you tend to use as a substitute for swearing. What should
   you say or think instead?

Footnotes

[1] The Index of Leading Cultural Indicators page 62.

[2] Linguistic Key, p. 535.

Thirteen

For everything there is a season

As Ecclesiastes says, there is a time for everything, including a time for your children to leave home. That time comes faster than you expect. Perhaps you will never feel "ready" for that day when your child walks out the door to live on his own, but you can prepare for it. You should be aiming for that goal from your children's youngest years.

As we already discussed in Chapter 8, Genesis 2 teaches that children should leave their home and begin a new one-flesh relationship away from their parents. Jesus quotes this passage in Matthew 19:4-5 and declares that it is still in force. This is the goal. The birth home is not a permanent place for children. In God's design, only the relationship of the husband and wife is permanent. Children are a vital part of that relationship, but their presence in the home is only temporary. Children are passing through. Your job, as we learned earlier, is to create a temporary greenhouse for your children to prepare them for the time when they will be on their own. Your job, parent, is to equip your children to move on, to begin a new family that will honor God. You should encourage them to plan for that day while they are still young.

Too often young people strike out on their own because home has become intolerable. You don't want that to happen. Rather, when your children do leave home you want them to go in peace. You want them to know the right time and direction they should take when they leave your home. This is the ultimate earthly goal of everyday talk. Here are a few practical implications.

Parents, your highest priority in life cannot be your children. As wonderful as children are, if they become the main focus of your life you will provide a distorted view of God's world for them. Your primary focus, of course, is to know and honor God. You must love and know God first and foremost. That is why Jesus sums up the commandments by saying that first you should love God with all that you are (Matt. 22:37-40). If this isn't what motivates you, you will not be able to exercise faith when difficult times come. Faith in man cannot sustain life. If your hopes and dreams are bound to your children or your spouse, you will be disappointed, perhaps even bitter. If you expect your spouse and/or your children to provide the comfort and support that can only come from God you will be deeply hurt. You will set yourself up to be disappointed and crushed when your family fails you. No spouse, no child can hope to provide comfort that can only be found in God. God will have no other gods before him. Your first loyalty must be to God and God alone.

After God, your husband or wife is to be the focus of your life. In Ephesians 5 husbands and wives are instructed to relate to each other as they would to the Lord. Husbands are to love their wives as Christ loves His church. Wives are to submit to their husbands as they would to the Lord. Many excellent books have been written about these passages, so I won't attempt to repeat them here. However, the point is that your spouse is to be the most important person in your life apart from God. God intends for your relationship with your spouse to be permanent in this life.

Children, then, come next. You are to train your children to know God and prepare to leave. Yet once again, things get turned around. Husbands and wives often spend time attempting to change each other—to train each other, if you will. When the spouse doesn't respond well to this "training," then some conclude it is time to leave. Children, on the other hand, may be accommodated and not trained, and parents may want them to stay forever. In the end, for far too many families, both the spouses and children leave and nothing is left but relational rubble.

Your everyday talk about preparing to leave is an important part of biblical training for your children. Many traps await parents as they live with their children. Some parents attempt to live out their own dreams through their children. Some parents seem to delight more in their children than they do in God or in their spouses. In other families, parents turn the exit light on earlier than they should. Sometimes parents are frustrated with their children's behavior and display no hope for their children. These actions and attitudes will influence your children to leave sooner than they should. Your everyday talk reflects your deepest attitudes and struggles. Examine your everyday talk carefully to make sure that you are not letting such attitudes creep into your life with your children.

Does your everyday talk prepare your children for leaving your home in such a way that they will be faithful servants of Christ? For most children, the door of safe exit from your home is the door that leads to marriage. That is not to say that children must marry immediately upon leaving your home. The Bible teaches that children should plan for and be ready for marriage as they leave, even if marriage is several years away (Proverbs

24:27).

For all young people, the door of safe exit must also lead to a good church.

Too often, parents just assume that their children will find the right church. That is a large assumption. What does your everyday talk reflect about your view of church? Does your everyday talk reveal a love for the institution that God has provided for your spiritual nurture? As your children and others listen to your unguarded comments about your church, what conclusions do they draw? Do you have good things to say about your pastor, your church leaders, your fellow members? Do your children have a view of the necessity of a good church that is consistent with God's view? Listen to what Paul says in Ephesians 4:11–14.

> He gave some as apostles, some as prophets, some as
> evangelists and some as shepherds and teachers, to equip
> the saints for a work of service leading to the building
> up of Christ's body until we all attain to the unity of the
> faith and to the full knowledge of God's Son, to mature
> manhood, to the point where we become as fully adult
> as Christ. This must happen so that we may no longer be
> infants, blown about and carried around by every wind
> of teaching, by human trickery, by craftiness designed to
> lead to error. (CCNT)

This familiar passage teaches many things. For our purpose, I want to focus on just one—the church is necessary to protect your children from the deceptions of this world. Paul says that the church was given so that Christians could reach maturity. Without the instruction of the church, your children will be prey to a deceptive world filled with human trickery and error. Without God's provision of His church, your children will think themselves to be wise adults ready to take on the world, but in reality they will be infants who will be led around by those who will cause them to fail miserably. That is what verse 14 means when it says, "This must happen so that . . . ." Protection from the hostile winds of the world comes in large part from being in a church that is following God and His Word. This is a vital message. Your everyday talk must reflect the reality that Ephesians 4 addresses. Do you want your children to leave home and be tossed about like a rag doll by a hostile world? No, of course not. God says that the stability they need will come from His church doing its work with them. Think about that.

When your children leave home they should have been trained already by your everyday talk to see how marriage and church will form vital building blocks of their lives away from your home.

You want to prepare your children to leave. Your everyday talk should help your children prepare to leave. Even if you lovingly and lightheartedly tell your kids that you never want them to leave (as we often have), you must also tell them what God wants for them. And since that is what God wants, that is what you want, too.

Application Questions

1. What does your everyday talk reflect about your view of church?

2. The world says that many alternative lifestyles are valid. What do your children believe about God's design for marriage and family?

3. How are you helping your children to be ready to leave your home?

Conclusion

Moses cried out to Israel to impress the things of God upon their hearts. Moses knew the words of God would bring Israel close to God. He reminded them that these words of God that he had spoken to them were their very life (Deuteronomy 32:47). Moses knew that if God's words were spoken and taught every day to God's people, life would flow abundantly. Moses knew that if Israel would love God enough to talk to their children about Him wherever they were, the nation would remain faithful to God. Solomon's words capture the impact of parents who take every opportunity to talk about God and His ways. The parent who faithfully follows Deuteronomy 6:7 can quote Proverbs 1:8–9 with confidence to his children. These words in Proverbs 1 are humbling words. Yet they also give great hope:

> Listen, my child, to what your father teaches you.
> Don't neglect your mother's teaching.
> What you learn from them will crown you with grace
> and clothe you with honor. (Proverbs 1:8-9)

No parent has all it takes to be worthy of the promise in these verses. However, when parents speak faithfully of God's ways and His holiness every day, the Holy Spirit uses the opportunity to apply the truth of Scripture to the young ears that hear it. Parents, God has given you a mission to make Him known in every corner of life. To pursue this mission takes great courage. As you walk along life's road with your children, you must literally deny yourself in order to speak first about God and how He views this world. When your child hears and learns about God this way he will indeed be clothed with honor and crowned with grace.

The challenge is great. The power of God is even greater. His power can make your everyday talk what He wants it to be—talk that reflects where your heart is, where your treasure is. Loving God means many things, but perhaps most profoundly it means loving Him so much that you speak of Him when you walk along the road, when you sit at home, when you lie down and when you get up.

John A. (Jay) Younts is a ruling elder serving at Redeemer Associate Reformed Presbyterian Church in Moore, SC. He is the author of *Finding the Right Track,* the *In Touch with Paul* Stewardship series, and *What About War.* He has studied and taught about biblical childrearing for 30 years. He and his wife Ruth have five children.

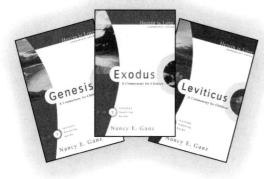

Shepherding a Child's Heart Resources

Don't Wait
Teach them the Gospel

"Presents the essential elements of the Gospel in an uncomplicated manner - explaining the truths of God, the Bible, Sin, Jesus, the need for Repentance and Faith, and Counting the Costs of the Christian life, but in a way little children will easily benefit from. " - Dr. Tedd Tripp

ISBN 09663786-8-7

This unusual book does something we sometimes take for granted; it methodically teaches the Gospel of Jesus Christ to young children, this is important because Romans 1:16 tells us the Gospel "is the power of God for the salvation of everyone who believes." It has a simple color picture for each Gospel Truth, and the entire picture collection at the end to help children recall these Truths. Hardcover. For ages 4 to 12.

In a handy quick-reference calendar style format *Wise Words for Moms* helps identify patterns of disobedience we find in our children and suggests examples of Scripture passages that will help address heart issues.

ISBN 09663786-6-0

www.shepherdpress.com
800-338-1445

Peacemaker Resources

The Young Peacemaker
By Corlette Sande

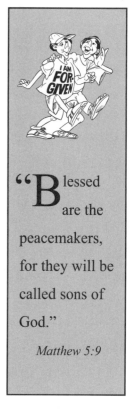

The Young Peacemaker curriculum is designed to teach children to prevent and resolve conflict by applying biblical principles of confession, forgiveness, communication, and character development. The use of realistic stories, practical applications, role plays, and stimulating activities makes this curriculum ideal for 8-12 year olds. Great home school or family resource. The teaching set includes a 12 lesson teacher manual and 12 reproducible Student Activity books.

"**B**lessed are the peacemakers, for they will be called sons of God."

Matthew 5:9

Teaching Set: Teacher's Manual + 12 different illustrated Activity Books. Item PR04: ISBN 0966378695 .... $29.95

Parent / Teacher Manual: ISBN 096637861X $19.95

Student Activity Book set (12): ISBN 096637862X ... $13.95

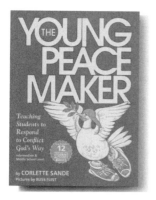